FAMILIES EXPERIENCING FAITH

A Parents' Guide to
the Young Adolescent Years

Janet Drey

THE WORLD OF
DON BOSCO
MULTIMEDIA

NEW ROCHELLE, NY

Families Experiencing Faith: A Parents' Guide to the Young Adolescent Years is published as part of the Catholic Families Series—resources to promote faith growth in Families.
Materials available for parish and diocesan leaders, parents and families

Available titles:

For leaders and ministers:
Families and Young Adults
Families and Youth
Families and Young Adolescents
Growing in Faith: A Catholic Family Sourcebook
Media, Faith, and Families: A Parish Ministry Guide
Rituals for Sharing Faith: A Resource for Parish Ministers
Faith and Families: A Parish Program for Parenting in Faith Growth

For parents and families:
Families Nurturing Faith: A Parents' Guide to the Preschool Years
Families Sharing Faith: A Parents' Guide to the Grade School Years
Families Exploring Faith: A Parents' Guide to the Older Adolescent Years
Families Encouraging Faith: A Parents' Guide to the Young Adult Years
Media, Faith, and Families: A Parents' Guide to Family Viewing
Family Rituals and Celebrations

The Catholic Families Series is a publishing project of Don Bosco Multimedia and the Center for Youth Ministry Development

Families Experiencing Faith: A Parents' Guide to the Young Adolescent Years
©1992 Salesian Society, Inc. / Don Bosco Multimedia
475 North Ave., P.O. Box T, New Rochelle, NY 10802
All rights reserved

Library of Congress Cataloging-in-Publication Data
Families Experiencing Faith: A Parents' Guide to the Young Adolescent Years / Janet Drey
p. cm. — Catholic Families Series
Includes bibliographical references.
    1. Family life 2. Religious development
      I. Drey, Janet
ISBN 0-89944-255-2 $6.95

Design and Typography by Sally Ann Zegarelli, Long Branch, NJ 07740

Printed in the United States of America

6/92   9 8 7 6 5 4 3 2 1

PREFACE

FAMILIES EXPERIENCING FAITH: A PARENTS' GUIDE TO THE YOUNG ADOLESCENT YEARS

A quick look at the family section of your local bookstore will reveal dozens of books about parenting. What you probably will not find among these titles is a book about parenting and faith growth. To fill this void, we have created five books which help parents of children from the pre-school years through the young adult years nurture the faith growth of their children. These new titles are part of the Catholic Families Series published by Don Bosco Multimedia.

Young adolescents are caught up in the challenges presented by puberty, new ways of thinking, an expanded circle of contacts and friends, growing autonomy, and the need to redefine family relationships. But they still need your concern and care. You can continue to have an influence on their faith and values, and grow with them in the process.

Families Experiencing Faith is specifically designed for parents of young adolescents. It provides you with an understanding of the unique characteristics of young adolescents and their families at this stage of life. It outlines the possibilities for sharing faith with young adolescents through the author's personal stories and through specific strategies and activities. It also suggests ways that you can continue your growth in faith.

Our hope is to promote opportunities for families with young adolescents to continue the faith sharing and faith growth which began in childhood. We hope you find the stories, insights and ideas a source of support and encouragement as you continue parenting.

ABOUT THE AUTHOR

Janet Drey is a specialist in ministry with young adolescents. She has served as a diocesan director of youth ministry. Janet is married and the mother of two children, one of whom is a young adolescent. She is author of another Catholic Family Series Book, *Families and Young Adolescents* and co-author of two youth programs in the Sadlier Youth Ministry Series, *Love and Lifestyles* and *Human Sexuality*.

CONTENTS

1

Parenting for Faith Growth Today
1

2

Understanding Families with Young Adolescents
21

3

Parenting Skills for Faith Growth
41

4

Strategies and Activities
61

1

PARENTING FOR FAITH GROWTH TODAY

WHY FAMILIES NEED FAITH

As every good parent knows, parenting involves much more than providing basic food and shelter, education and health care. Parenting is also about loving and caring, building self-esteem and a sense of values. Effective parenting helps children understand how they relate to others and what they can do to make the world a better place for themselves and for all people.

Parenting is a shared task. Despite all the different shapes that families come in today—single-parent and two-parent, blended and extended—the challenge of parenting continues to be shared across generations and across family lines. Grandparents, aunts and cousins share in the task, as do special friends who have become "family" for us in a different way. People of faith proclaim that God is also an active partner with them in their job of parenting.

Faith provides family members with shared beliefs and values to guide their life together and to direct their involvement beyond the family circle. Faith values nurture the family's well-being and provide it with the criteria needed to weigh and evaluate the many messages that come its way each day. Faith proclaims, for example, that every person is endowed by God with dignity and blessed with a unique mix of gifts and talents. These gifts and talents, in turn, are meant to be shared with others. This vision of personhood calls families to recognize, nurture and celebrate the uniqueness of each family member. It also calls families to recognize their interdependence with others and to share the talents and gifts nurtured in family life with others in their community and world. As simple as this faith value seems, it often stands in sharp contrast to societal messages that judge people in light of what they have or that promote isolation from others who seem, at least at first glance, to be different from us.

As parents model faith values at home and in the community, nurture a sense of dignity and uniqueness in their children and encourage family members to share their talents with others, they join with God in the sacred task of building a world based on gospel values. Children, in turn, take what they have learned and practiced at home and carry it into the world, guaranteeing a new generation committed to creating a world based on gospel values.

Faith serves, as well, as a source of comfort and strength for parents, assuring them that they are not alone in the task of parenting and providing them with a special Friend to whom they can turn for direction and support. As parents join with their God in the task of parenting, they come to realize that there are no social, geographical or educational barriers to good parenting. Good parenting does not depend upon a high hourly wage, a prestigious address or the number of degrees after a person's name. You don't have to be a biological parent to develop a strong family life. You can be an adoptive parent, a single parent, a parent of healthy or handicapped children. Good parenting is possible for all people who trust enough in themselves, in the other members of their families and in their God.

Faith provides people with the values and vision needed to live life fully. Families need faith to survive and thrive in today's world. Our challenge in this book is to offer you and your family practical insights and strategies for developing a meaningful faith life.

KEYS TO EFFECTIVE PARENTING

Before we begin this book on parenting for faith growth and turn to the descriptions and suggestions offered by our author, it will be important to look at the adventure of parenting today and what we mean by parenting for faith growth.

As noted above, the key to effective parenting lies within you. Your drive to make your family the best that it can be need not be blocked by your particular life circumstances. To be sure, your path may be more winding and littered than some, but effectiveness in parenting is an internal quality, not easily squashed by external conditions. It is a desire to make the most of yourself and your family, whatever your talents or situation.

What do we know about effective parenting? Who can we turn to for advice? One of the best sources for our wisdom about parenting is to turn to other parents. In *Back to the Family*, Dr. Ray Guarendi gathered the shared wisdom of one hundred of America's happiest and most effective families. He shares the following thoughts on what makes families effective:[1]

1. **A strong home life does not depend upon a parent's education, occupation, ethnicity or social status.** Neither is it limited to biological parents, two-parent homes or a low-stress existence. Effective parenting and a strong home life are not

the product of external causes but are born internally. They evolve from commitment, from determination to build upon your family's strengths, regardless of what factors may be pulling against you.

2. Successful parents are not all products of successful childhoods. While many parents knew upbringings filled with positive examples from which to anchor their own parenting, others have lived through childhoods best described as cold, abusive or even traumatic. Parents who have risen far above their childhoods are living proof that, contrary to some experts' opinions, the quality of your past does not put a ceiling on the quality of your present as a parent or as a person.

3. Effective parents are not perfect or even close to perfect. They wrestle with worries, insecurities and guilts all parents feel. They don't have all the answers, endless patience or perfect children. Their lives reveal that skillful parenting is not inborn. It is developed over time, along with a healthy acceptance of one's imperfections. Better parenting results from recognizing our limits and working to overcome them or live with them.

4. Good parents love to parent. They've experienced the challenges and fears inherent to childrearing and remain grateful for the opportunity to be parents. Lifestyles and priorities can change radically with the decision to raise children. Responsible parents accept this reality, even welcome it.

5. Common sense and good judgment form the foundation for sound parenting decisions. Having discovered that no one right way exists for handling any situation, effective parents strive for self-confidence. It leads to more decisive parenting and more secure children. Childrearing is a never-ending process. It is drawing upon the knowledge and experience of others—children, parents and experts. The willingness to learn from others is indispensable to better parenting, but ultimately you must judge for yourself what

A PARENTS' GUIDE TO THE YOUNG ADOLESCENT YEARS

- *Parent in the present.* Second guessing yourself or dwelling on the uncertain future will erode your confidence and ability to give your best to your children today.
- *Expect that your children will misunderstand and dislike you at times.* That is a reality of responsible parenthood.
- *Laugh whenever and wherever you can during childrearing.* Humor helps maintain perspective and eases anxiety.

9. Spiritual beliefs are a dominant presence in strong families. Faith in a Creator and in living by God's guidelines provide values which nurture each member's personal growth and thereby the family's. Spirituality fosters parenting through example, the most durable parenting. It is a source of comfort and strength, enabling parents to call upon a supreme authority for wisdom and direction.

10. There are no shortcuts to strong family life. A parent must invest time. Dedication means a willingness to give quantity time, which is necessary for quality time. Time provides the framework for all elements of family success—communication, discipline, values. Making family a priority fosters a child's self-esteem and sense of belonging. Nothing is more precious to a child than the presence of a parent.

11. Competent parents concentrate on mastering the basics of communication. A few good principles guide them:

- *Talk less at children and listen more to them.* Attentive silence is the simplest way to evoke a child's feelings.
- *Become sensitive to children's prime times to talk.* Arrange them or be present when they occur. They are windows into their thoughts.
- *Affection is continuous communication.* It is love without words. Strong families know the binding power of affection.

- *Whenever possible, allow children a voice in family decisions.* While in most cases, parents retain the final say, merely being consulted makes a child feel an integral part of the family.

12. Responsible parents expect much of their children and of themselves. Their attitude is, "Success is not measured against others but against yourself. Striving for your personal best is a success." Parents counsel:

- *Insist on your children's full effort in academics.* It is their future.

- *The family home is everyone's home, so make it everyone's responsibility*, down to the youngest members.

- *Judge children's capabilities—social, emotional, personal—and expect them to live up to them.* Don't allow them to live down to the norm.

13. Strong parents believe in strong discipline begun young. They are willing to exert whatever effort is necessary to discipline their children today so life won't discipline them tomorrow. The firmest parent, if loving, is a more gentle teacher than the world. For a child's sake, parents need the will to discipline. The best discipline is motivated by unconditional love, love that is unaffected by a child's misbehavior. Good disciplinarians focus most on what children do right, not wrong. They emphasize the positive. Not only does this make for less discipline, it enhances a child's self image. By their nature, children test limits and want more than is healthy for them. Loving parents are not afraid to say no. They draw clear boundaries within which a child is free to operate.

The mechanics of effective discipline are summarized by the three C's: calm, consistency and consequences. Calm discipline works more quickly and leads to less regrettable behavior from everyone. Consistency is predictability. It enables children to understand and accept the results of their actions. Consequences, not words, are the basic tools of discipline.

14. Strong families rely on simple, clear-cut home rules enforced by consequences. They derive some of their stability from house rules. Established according to a family's needs and goals, rules make for a more content household. The content of the rules changes as the family evolves, but their purpose remains the constant: to promote mutual respect, responsibility and a more pleasant environment for everyone.

Refined to its most basic elements, successful parenting is unconditional love, commitment, teaching by example and the will to discipline. Effective parenting is an attainable reality. Build upon the essentials, and no level of family success is beyond your reach. In this book we will be encouraging you to utilize these ingredients of effective parenting by suggesting practical insights and skills for parenting young adults.

THE FAMILY AS A LIVING SYSTEM

No human being grows in a vacuum. To be human is, by definition, to be interdependent, to rely on others for the support and assistance needed to grow to full life. No place is this more apparent than in the life of the family. Family members depend upon one another and have a tremendous impact on one another's growth. Change and growth in any family member's life automatically impacts all other family members. If a major change occurs in the life of a single family member, all members are forced to adjust to the change. This can entail adjustments in the relationships among individual family members or a recasting of what it means to be family together.

Researchers use the term "system" to describe the organic relationship that exists between individual family members and the family as a whole. You may remember from high school science classes that living organisms and their environments function as a system. All living systems attempt to maintain *equilibrium* or balance. When a change takes place that upsets this balance, the system responds by doing something to restore the equilibrium that existed previously.

The family is a system, too—a system in which relationships change in response to the changing needs and concerns of family members and in response to changes in the family's relationship with the larger society. And like other systems, families attempt to maintain a sense of equilibrium in their relationships. Certain understandings develop regarding roles, rules, relationships and responsibilities in the family. These understandings form the system by which the family operates. Often times, families are unaware of how these roles, rules, relationships and responsibilities affect their entire life as a family.

The tendency for family systems to try to maintain their established patterns of behavior is challenged from time to time by changes to which they must adapt. These changes can be a regular part of the family's growth and development. The birth of the first child causes an imbalance in the family system of the couple, often making many of the former roles, rules, relationships and responsibilities unworkable. The arrival of adolescence brings with it periods of imbalance as formerly accepted roles, rules, relationships and responsibilities are questioned by the adolescent. During these life transitions it is *healthy* for family roles, rules, relationships and responsibilities to change, for through such changes families adjust to the changes and restore a new balance to the system.

Sometimes these changes are brought about by major events in the life of the family, such as the loss of a parent through death or divorce or the remarriage of parents resulting in a new blended family. The members of a family must find ways to reorganize and reestablish workable roles, rules, relationships and responsibilities in light of these major life events. Such changes often result in longer periods of imbalance as the family system seeks to adjust to the changes and establish a new balance. Making changes during these major events is difficult, but it is *healthy*. Families need to adjust to the new situation they face and restore a new balance to the system. Only in this way can the family feel comfortable again.

At other times, you as the parent may wish to make a change in the family by introducing new ways of relating, new patterns of family living, new rules, new practices, etc. In this book we introduce you to a variety of ways to share faith with your children. You may want to use many of these new ideas in your family. Be aware that family members often resist change, not because the changes are bad, but because change is upsetting. It causes anxiety. When a family establishes its balance, members are comfortable with the status quo. Anything new, even if positive, will likely be resisted, and a subtle message of "change back" will be communicated. Change requires at least three steps: the change itself, the family's reaction to the change and dealing with the family's reaction to the change. By understanding how your family system works (what the roles, rules, relationship patterns and responsibilities are), you can be prepared for your family's reaction. For example, you can identify what needs to change in order to introduce the idea, involve family members in deciding and planning for the change, keep communication lines open during the change, suggest that they try the new idea for a specific length of time and then evaluate, etc.

HOW FAMILIES GROW

Today it has become commonplace to talk about the changes we experience throughout our lives. We are aware of the differing life tasks and characteristics of childhood, adolescence, young adulthood, middle adulthood and later adulthood. Each of these "stages" or times of life brings with it new challenges and important life tasks to accomplish. In a family both children and parents are experiencing their own individual journeys.

We may not be as fully aware that the family as a unit or system has important life tasks to address and needs and functions to fulfill. A family in its "infancy" is different from a family in its "adolescence." Like individuals, families move through a life cycle, a family life cycle—that is, various stages in which new issues arise and different concerns predominate. During the first years of marriage, for example, families focus nearly all their energy on establishing a household, finding suitable employment and strengthening the marital relationship. During the child-bearing stage, the family's concerns shift to taking care of their young children. Families are likely to have higher medical expenses, more debts in general and concerns about managing work and family commitments. During the "young adult" stage, when children begin leaving home, families are usually less strained financially, and their concerns shift to reorganizing the household in response to their children's departure. Each stage of the family life cycle is different from those that came before and those that will follow.

These family life cycle changes are a regular part of the family's growth and development. Consequently, in order to understand the changing nature of family relationships throughout the family life cycle, we must take into account not only characteristics of the developing child or adolescent or young adult, but characteristics of the parents and of the family as a system at each stage of life.

A family life cycle perspective sees the family as a three or four generational system moving through time in a life cycle of distinct stages. During each stage the family is confronted with particular tasks to accomplish and challenges to face in order to prepare itself and its members for further growth and development. Viewing family life through a systems perspective can be a powerful tool for helping people understand what is happening in the life of their family and for creating strategies that promote individual and family faith growth and sharing.

Starting with the new couple, the following brief paragraphs describe the tasks faced by families at each stage of development. While no single development theory can explain all the factors that contribute to individual and family growth, such theories do provide windows through which we can gain a better understanding of how families change and grow. They help us understand what is happening in the life of the individual and in the life of the family as a whole.[2]

NEW COUPLE

Marriage joins not just two individuals, but two families together in a new relationship. It presents the new couple with a series of new challenges, including:

- defining and learning the role of husband and wife;
- establishing new relationships as a couple with their families of origin and with their friends;
- developing a commitment to a new family, with its own rules, roles, responsibilities, values and traditions.

As they confront these challenges, the new couple often finds themselves reflecting on the influence of their family of origin to draw insights, values and traditions that they want to include in their new family. This reflection helps them to sort out emotionally what they will take along from the family of origin, what they will leave behind and what they will create for themselves.

FAMILIES WITH CHILDREN

With the birth of the first child, the couple embarks on a new life task—to accept new members into the family and to adjust the rules, roles, responsibilities and relationships of their family to include the needs of the youngest members. The challenge for families with children involves:

- developing parenting roles and skills;
- negotiating and joining in childrearing, financial and household tasks;
- realigning relationships with extended family to include grandparenting roles;
- sharing socialization with the outside world;

- developing new patterns of family communication, traditions, celebrations.

FAMILIES WITH ADOLESCENTS

Adolescence ushers in a new era in family life brought on by new adolescent life tasks and the changing role of the parents in relationship to their adolescent children. The changes of adolescence—puberty, new ways of thinking, wider sphere of social activity and relationships, greater autonomy—present the family as a whole with a new set of challenges. In fact, it would be fair to say that the whole family experiences adolescence. The challenge for families with adolescents involves:

- allowing for the increasing independence of adolescents, while maintaining enough structure to foster continued family development;
- reflection by adult members on their personal, marital and career life issues;
- adjusting patterns of family communication, traditions, celebrations;
- and for some families beginning the shift toward joint caring for the older generation.

The task for most families with adolescents—and it is by no means an easy one—is to maintain *emotional* involvement, in the form of concern and caring, while gradually moving toward a relationship characterized by greater *behavioral* autonomy.

FAMILIES WITH YOUNG ADULTS

The most significant aspect of this stage of life is that it is marked by the greatest number of exits and entries of family members. The stage begins with the launching of grown children into schooling, careers and homes of their own,

and proceeds with the entry of their spouses and children. The challenge for families with young adults involves:
- regrouping as a family as each young adult moves out from the family;
- changes in the marital relationship now that parenting responsibilities are no longer required;
- development of adult-to-adult relationships between grown children and their parents;
- realigning relationships to include in-laws and grandchildren;
- caring for the older generation and dealing with disabilities and death.

This stage of family life also presents unique challenges to the young adult, for example:
- accepting emotional and financial responsibility for oneself;
- formulating personal life goals;
- developing intimate peer relationships;
- establishing oneself in the world of work.

FAMILIES IN LATER LIFE

Among the tasks of families in later life is the adjustment to retirement, which not only may create the obvious vacuum for the retiring person, but may put a special strain on the marriage. Financial insecurity and dependence are also special difficulties, especially for family members who value managing for themselves. And while loss of friends and relatives is a particular difficulty at this phase, the loss of a spouse is the most difficult adjustment, with its problems of reorganizing one's entire life alone after many years as a couple and of having fewer relationships to help replace the loss. Grandparenthood can, however, offer a new lease on life and opportunities for special close relationships without the responsibilities of parenthood.

In this book we will describe many of the major characteristics and concerns of the growing young adolescent, as well as those of parents and the family as a whole. These explanations will help you to understand the changing nature of family relationships during adolescence and to offer practical suggestions for parenting and faith growth in families with young adolescents.

HOW FAMILIES GROW IN FAITH

The Christian vision of family life speaks about the family as a community of life and love. It proclaims that family life is sacred and that family activities are holy, that God's love is revealed and communicated in new ways each and every day through Christian families. This Christian vision of family life calls families to a unique identity and mission. This means that the Christian family has several important responsibilities as it seeks to grow in faith:

- *Families form a loving community.*
  Families work to build a community based on love, compassion, respect, forgiveness and service to others. In families, people learn how to give and receive love and how to contribute to the good of other family members. In families, people open themselves to experiencing God's love through their dealings with one another, through the ethnic and cultural values and traditions that are part of family life and through the events of family life.

- *Families serve life by bearing and educating children.*
  Families serve life by bringing children into the world, by handing on Catholic Christian values and traditions and by developing the potential of each member at every age. As parents and all family members share their values with one another, they grow toward moral and spiritual maturity.

- *Families participate in building a caring and just society.*
  Families participate in building a caring and just society.

The gospel values of service, compassion and justice are first learned and practiced in families. In Christian families people learn how to reach out beyond the home to serve those in need and to work for justice for all God's people. How family members learn to relate to each other with respect, love, caring, fidelity, honesty and commitment becomes their way of relating to others in the world.

- *Families share in the life and mission of the Church.*
Families share in the life and mission of the Church when the gospel vision and values are communicated and applied in daily life, when faith is celebrated through family rituals or through participation in the sacramental life of the church, when people gather as a family or parish community to pray, when people reach out, in Jesus' name, in loving service to others.

These responsibilities may sound overwhelming and unrealistic given all your other responsibilities as parents. In this book we will use these four responsibilities to develop practical ideas that you can use to share faith and promote individual and family faith growth. We will organize our ideas around six time-honored ways of sharing faith: (1) sharing the Catholic faith story, (2) celebrating faith through rituals, (3) praying together, (4) enriching family relationships, (5) responding to those in need through actions of justice and service, and (6) relating to the wider community.

Sharing the Catholic faith story happens when parents share stories from the Scriptures with their children, when families discuss the implications and applications of Christian faith for daily living, when a moral dilemma is encountered and the family turns to the resources of the Catholic faith for guidance, when parents discuss the religious questions their young adolescents ask. The family's sharing is complemented by participation of children, parents and/or the entire family in the catechetical program of the parish community.

Celebrating faith through rituals happens when the family celebrates the liturgical year, such as Advent and

Christmas, Lent and Easter; celebrates the civic calendar, like Martin Luther King, Jr. Day and Earth Day; celebrates milestones or rites of passages, such as birthdays, anniversaries, graduations, special recognitions; celebrates ethnic traditions which have been passed down through the generations; celebrates the rituals of daily life, like meal prayer and forgiveness. These celebrations provide the foundations for a family ritual life in which God is discovered and celebrated through the day, week, month and year. The family's ritual life is complemented by participation in the ritual life of the parish community with its weekly celebration of the Eucharist; regular sacramental celebrations, such as Reconciliation and Anointing of the Sick; and liturgical year celebrations.

Praying together as a family is a reality when families incorporate prayer into the daily living through meal and bed times, times of thanksgiving and of crisis; when parents teach basic prayers and pray with their children. The family's prayer life is complemented by participation in the communal prayer life of the parish community, especially through liturgical year celebrations.

Enriching family relationships occurs when the family spends both quality and quantity time together; participates in family activities; works at developing healthy communication patterns which cultivate appreciation, respect and support for each other; negotiates and resolves problems and differences in positive and constructive ways. Enriching family relationships also involves the parents in developing their marriage relationship or a single parent developing intimate, supportive relationships in his or her life.

Performing acts of justice and service takes place when the family recognizes the needs of others in our communities and in our world and seeks to respond. Families act through stewardship and care for the earth; through direct service to others, the homeless and the hungry; through study of social issues; through developing a family lifestyle based on equality, nonviolence, respect for human dignity, respect for the earth. The family's service involvement is strengthened when it is done together with other families in the parish community.

Relating as a family to the wider community happens when families join together in family support groups or family clusters for sharing, activities and encouragement; when families learn about the broader church and world, especially the cultural heritages of others in the community or the world; when families organize to address common concerns facing them in the community, like quality education or safe neighborhoods.

This is quite a challenge for the family! Don't be overwhelmed. What is essential is that you identify how you already share faith using these six ways and try new approaches that will enrich your family life. In this book we have included ideas to support your current efforts and to encourage you to try new ways to share faith. Adapt and revise these ideas so that they work for you.

Remember that the family shares responsibility with the parish community for promoting faith growth in each of these six ways. A careful look at the six ways will reveal the basic functions of the parish community, e.g., religious education, sacraments and worship, serving the needs of others. The parish and family approach each of these six ways of sharing faith differently. The parish community needs to support and encourage the efforts of families to share faith. Families need to be involved in the life of the parish community so that their family efforts can be connected to the larger community of faith. Don't be afraid to challenge your parish community and its leaders to support families and to offer programs and services for families that will promote the family's growth in faith.

GROWING TOWARD MATURITY IN FAITH

What do we hope will happen in the lives of family members—parents and children alike—if we strengthen our efforts at sharing faith? It is our hope that family members will discover meaning and purpose for their lives in a life-transforming relationship with a loving God in Jesus Christ and a consistent devotion to serving others as Jesus did.

Our growth as Catholic Christians is never complete. It is a life-long journey towards greater maturity in faith. While no complete description of this journey is possible, we hope and pray that you and your family will grow toward a living faith characterized by the following elements:

- trusting in God's saving grace and firmly believing in the humanity and divinity of Jesus Christ;
- experiencing a sense of personal well-being, security and peace;
- integrating faith and life—seeing work, family, social relationships and political choices as part of your religious life;
- seeking spiritual growth through Scripture, study, reflection, prayer and discussion with others;
- seeking to be part of a Catholic community of believers in which people give witness to their faith, support and nourish one another, serve the needs of each other and the community, and worship together;
- developing a deeper understanding of the Catholic Christian tradition and its applicability to life in today's complex society;
- holding life-affirming gospel values, including respect for human dignity, commitment to uphold human rights, equality (especially racial and gender), stewardship, care and compassion and a personal sense of responsibility for the welfare of others;
- advocating for social and global change to bring about greater social justice and peace;
- serving humanity, consistently and passionately, through acts of love and justice.

Families provide a natural context for nurturing God's gift of faith. As families and individuals grow together in faith, life is enriched and the gospel vision brought closer to reality. Faith and family are a natural duo. May this volume be one small step toward helping you grow together more effectively.

End Notes

[1] These points about effective parenting were summarized from *Back to the Family* by Ray Guarendi (New York: Villard Books, 1990).

[2] The family life cycle perspective described below was adapted from "The Family Life Cycle," by Betty Carter and Monica McGoldrick in *Growing in Faith: A Catholic Family Sourcebook,* ed. John Roberto (New Rochelle: Don Bosco Multimedia, 1990.)

2

UNDERSTANDING FAMILIES WITH YOUNG ADOLESCENTS

Nothing seems to strike fear in the hearts of parents more than the realization that their child is becoming an ADOLESCENT! But, contrary to popular belief, that doesn't mean that you will suddenly grow apart or start fighting all the time. Adolescence can also be a time of family togetherness and healthy dialogue. There are many myths about adolescents, none of which you should necessarily believe. Two of the most prevalent, which we have found to be untrue are:

1. Adolescents and parents fight all the time.

2. Adolescents are rebellious by nature.

To be sure, adolescents and their parents do have difficulties—but, then again, so do young children and their parents, and so do adults and their parents. When teenagers and their parents differ, it is most likely to be over day-to-day interests, such as styles of dress or taste in music, rather than fundamental issues such as long-term educational or occupational plans. It is not so much the actual conflicts, though, but how they are handled—and how they have been handled over time—that will determine how the adolescent relates to his or her family.

Adolescence is a time of change and challenge, but most young people (and adults!) survive it without serious problems. If children feel good about their family life, everything else about being a young adolescent will be a little bit easier. For parents, adolescence can be much more than a time of "problems"—it can also be a time of great pride as young adolescents grow in their new abilities, independent thinking and sense of self.

In order to understand families with young adolescents, let us examine first the changes that occur in them as individual family members, and then the new tasks and the adjustment required of the family. What changes happen during this time? How should the other family members adapt in response to them?

CHANGES IN YOUNG ADOLESCENTS

PUBERTY

You don't have to be around young adolescents very long to realize that physical and sexual development play a central role in the changes that are occurring in their lives. Biologically, young adolescents grow more rapidly than at any other time in their lives except infancy. Most young adolescents are excited about the physical changes that are happening to their bodies, but at the same time they are often concerned about whether their bodies are normal and how they will look when their bodies are mature. Adjusting to these changes and altered expectations from others, along with the hormones raging through their bodies, can make young adolescents vulnerable to bouts of low self-esteem, moodiness, and intense emotion.

Adolescence, at least physiologically, begins much earlier than many parents think. By age 10 or so, the average child has entered puberty, during which his or her childish body will be transformed into that of a mature man or woman, capable of reproduction. The outward signs of sexual maturation, however, may not appear for several years.

In childhood, growth is slow and steady; in puberty, it is rapid and dramatic. During the adolescent growth spurt, the average young person grows twelve inches in height and gains twenty to thirty pounds. It's not unusual for a boy or girl to grow three to five inches in a single year, literally bursting out of last season's clothes. To complicate matters, all parts of the body do not grow at the same time or rate. Typically, the hands and feet spurt before the arms and legs; the arms and legs before the torso. If adolescents feel awkward and gawky, it is because their bodies *are, temporarily,* out of proportion, and there is nothing they can do to speed up or slow down the process.

No wonder young people in the throes of puberty sometimes feel that their bodies are out of control, that they will never start (or stop) growing and that everything about the way they look is wrong. An urgent question for many adolescents is, "Am I normal?" Virtually all are. Making sure that your teenagers have plenty of information about what to expect from their changing bodies and emotions, even if it makes you uncomfortable, will relieve some of their anxieties.

At a stage when young people want more than anything to be like everyone else, they find themselves the *least* alike. Everyone their age is growing and changing, but each at his or her own pace. For a start, girls show the outward signs of development two years earlier, on the average, than boys do. In sixth grade, a girl may tower over boys her age.

Differences within each sex are just as great. Some girls begin to develop as early as age eight and others as late as age 13; in boys the outward signs of puberty may appear at age 10 or not until age 14 or 15. Some young people race through puberty in a year and a half, while others take five or six years to mature. This means that one teenager may complete puberty before another the same age begins. Best friends may look and feel worlds apart. Because young people often compare themselves to each other, they can easily forget that no one can help the way that he or she is growing. As parents, we need to remember that there may be wide variations in "normal" growth rates during puberty. As much as a six-year span in physical development can exist between a quickly-developing girl and a slowly-developing boy. A group of 12- or 13-year-olds would probably include some girls who look like young women and are capable of bearing children as well as girls who are just beginning to develop womanly curves and are not menstruating. A few boys in the group might look like strapping young men while others have barely begun their growth spurt. Because girls tend to go through puberty a year or two ahead of boys the same age, this may lead to some attractions between boys and girls that are worrisome for parents.

Finally, puberty follows an independent biological timetable which bears little relation to other aspects of maturation. A girl may look like a woman long before she feels like one inside. A boy may be mature in almost every way but still look like a child. We need to be sure that our expectations are in line with our children's abilities: not too high if they "look" old or too low if they are not maturing as fast as some of their peers.

Young adolescents need time to stretch, wiggle and exercise their rapidly growing bodies. They need lots of physical activity but also time to rest and relax. Because of the diversity in strength, dexterity and size of young adolescents, though, intense competition can often reward early bloomers and place an unnecessary burden on late-bloomers who cannot compete successfully. (It can be depressing to always be picked last for basketball games in gym just because you are the shortest in the class.)

Young people hunger for chances to prove themselves, especially in ways that are rewarding if all goes well and not devastating if there are some disappointments. Young adolescents need to know that who they are and what they do is valued by their parents and by others whom they respect. Helping young adolescents find new areas of strength and giving lots of praise and positive reinforcement for their efforts goes a long way to bolster their sometimes tenuous self-esteem.

NEW WAYS OF THINKING

Young adolescents are applying new thinking skills to the issues and situations they face in life. Family rules and beliefs that used to be taken for granted are now openly and regularly questioned. The intellectual growth spurt of adolescence involves new ways of thinking, and unless parents know what to expect, the shift from immature thinking to abstract ideas, hypothetical situations and formal logic is easy to misinterpret and can cause conflict between teenagers and their parents.

Between the ages of ten and fourteen years, young adolescents begin to develop the capacity to think abstractly, but they show much diversity in this area. Some young people may be mastering the new thinking skills referred to as "formal operations," but most are still moving between the concrete thinking of childhood and the abstract thinking that is more characteristic of adulthood. To make things even more complicated, your child may be able to think abstractly in one area of his or her life but not in another. Adolescents who insist on thinking things through for themselves one day may want someone to just tell them what to do the next day. And, the growing ability to think logically won't instantly lead to consistency between thoughts and actions. Although this may be frustrating, it is normal; changes in young adolescents' thinking abilities occur gradually.

In the process of trying out their new thinking skills, young adolescents often ask to help plan family activities and guidelines. It is important to include them for a number of reasons. First, it is one way that they will begin to learn to make decisions and where better than in the safety of the family? Second, the more input—with adult guidance—that teenagers have in helping decide family rules, the more likely they will be to respect and follow those rules. It is crucial for young people who may imagine themselves to be invulnerable to dangerous risks to have solid guidelines to follow, with clear and predictable and swift consequences if they don't. Regardless of family structure, parents need to agree on basic guidelines and support one another in the task of parenting young adolescents. How this gets worked out from family to family will differ, but the goal remains the same—to provide consistent direction and support for young people as they take increased personal responsibility for their decisions and actions.

Abstract Concepts

Intellectually, children and teenagers are worlds apart. Preadolescent children think in terms of concrete actions and events; only things they can see and touch really have meaning to them. Being religious to a child, for instance, means going to church on Sunday. To an adolescent, however, for whom abstract concepts like justice, honesty and loyalty are taking on new meaning, being religious becomes something you *believe in*, not just something you *do*. These abstractions add a new layer to the young person's thinking. The simple black-and-white world of childhood, where everyone is good or bad, mean or nice, smart or stupid, gives way to gray expanses of uncertainty, ambiguity and debate. It adds even more complexity to an age where figuring the world out is already difficult enough, but it also makes life more interesting.

Possibilities

These increasing intellectual abilities open adolescents to many new possibilities. For adolescents, what is real (what exists now) is only one of many possibilities (what could or might exist). They can suddenly conceive of a world without war, a society without adults or life with a different set of parents. Thinking about possibilities raises the issue of identity, and adolescents begin to think about how their personalities and social lives might change in the future. To children, you are who you are: Identity is given. To adolescents, who you are now is only one of many possibilities. It is part of their job on their journey through adolescence to try on new personalities, gestures, moods, hairdos, clothing styles and philosophies to see how they feel and what "fits." Visionaries and idealists one day, adolescents can be harsh social critics the next. Their harshest criticism is often directed at the ones who are nearest and dearest—themselves, their friends, their parents and trusted adults. It is hard, but try to be patient. Being a young adolescent is hard work!

The Imaginary Audience

One of the major intellectual advances of adolescence is the ability to think about what others are thinking ("He knows that I know that he knows..."). Unfortunately, this revelation can become an obsession; teenagers often imagine that everyone else is always thinking about them! In effect, they construct an "imaginary audience" that observes and evaluates their every move. When the family goes out to dinner, a daughter slouches in the darkest corner, terrified that her friends will see what weirdos she has for parents. If you can imagine trying to work or give a small, intimate dinner party in a department store window, you'll know how self-conscious your young adolescent feels much of the time.

The Personal Fable

The feeling that one is the center of attention can lead to feelings of exaggerated self-importance. In young adolescence this takes the form of a personal fable. The adolescent sees herself as unique and special; social rules and natural laws that apply to other people do not apply to her. She is invulnerable, invincible, immortal. On an abstract level, young adolescents understand that playing with drugs can lead to addiction or an overdose; sex without contraception, to pregnancy; driving above the speed limit, to a ticket or an accident. But they do not have the intellectual capacity to integrate this abstract knowledge into their life. As one parent put it, her teenager, "actually believes that he won't get acne because he is philosophically opposed to pimples."

Adolescents' feelings of uniqueness lead them to honestly believe that no one has ever loved as deeply, hurt as badly or understood things as clearly as they do. Respecting the depth of their feelings is essential, even when you disagree on the importance of the concerns in which they have invested their feelings.

Apparent Hypocrisy

Young adolescents can appear extraordinarily hypocritical. They expound lofty principles one minute, violate those same principles the next, then become indignant if an adult points out the discrepancy between their words and deeds. A teenager may lambaste a parent or adult for caring too much about appearances, then hop in the shower or change his clothes for the third time that day. Another teenager and a friend may spend hours talking about how they can't *stand* so-and-so because she's such a gossip. This apparent hypocrisy is the result of intellectual immaturity, not moral weakness. Unlike some adults, whom we can assume are aware of the connection between theory and practice, young adolescents have difficulty making this connection.

Overthinking

Young adolescents can get carried away with their new-found ability to grasp complexities and may overlook obvious, simple solutions to a problem. One reason young adolescents have so much trouble making decisions, for example, is that they are able to contemplate innumerable possibilities. Deciding what to wear or what to order in a restaurant can be agonizing, because there are so many choices. Your daughter may be so caught up in how many different looks she could put together that she literally *can't* decide what to buy or what to wear to a party two weeks later. Being able to hold many variables in mind simultaneously is an important skill, one that will help your adolescent in history and math classes now and in business later on. But in early adolescence, young people have difficulty knowing when advanced thinking is appropriate and when it is unnecessary and counterproductive.

A GROWING CONCERN WITH PERSONAL APPEARANCE

Parents often complain that their adolescents spend hours in front of the mirror. Young adolescents can be painfully self-conscious of their rapidly changing bodies and what others think of them. Likewise, their minds need time to absorb new ways of thinking, new mirrored reflections and new reactions from others. To accommodate the new people they are becoming, young adolescents need time to see and reflect on all of these new things and "absorb" their new body image, glasses, facial hair and all that is happening inside and all around them.

Young adolescents also need parents who like and respect them for who they are *right now*. They look to parents to reassure them and to respond sensitively to their present joys and confusion, and their dreams and worries for the future. They need many non-judgmental opportunities to express their new feelings, interests, abilities and thoughts to help them understand and accept the new people they are becoming.

Young adolescents can have strong reactions to statements from parents and other adults that begin with, "When you grow up..." What is real for them is *now* and that is where they need us to be with them.

DEVELOPING A NEW SENSE OF RIGHT AND WRONG

All parents want to help teenagers develop a strong set of values and the courage to stand up for what they believe is right. In adolescence, this sometimes seems like an uphill battle. TV soap operas and serials, movies and many popular books treat violence, law-breaking and casual sex as normal, acceptable events.

Young adolescents, to a large extent, make their moral judgments by what is expected of them by family, peers and other persons significant in their lives. They want to live up to the expectations of people they know and care about. They can now empathize with others and imagine how they would feel if they lost five dollars, were left out of a game or were pushed around by a bully. They see the limitations of getting even and understand that, "Two wrongs don't make a right." They *want* to please and, above all, they want others to like them.

That is fine when the people the child is trying to please set high moral standards, but what if the audience applauds deception rather than honesty, defiance rather than cooperation, risk-taking rather than self-respect, snobbery and sarcasm rather than generosity and kindness?

When the "good boy/nice girl" level of moral reasoning first appears in mid- to late elementary school, parents are delighted. The child seems more caring, more cooperative and generally easier to live with. The reason? She is eager to please her parents. In junior high, however, the same child may suddenly seem sullen, uncooperative and rebellious. The reason? She is now more interested in pleasing her peers. At this age, moral decisions are likely to be based on what she thinks will make her popular. "But Mom, *everybody* does it," is a common refrain. A girl who was nice to a shy, friendless child in sixth grade because she had been taught to be kind, may turn clannish and cruel in eighth grade to maintain her status with her peers. One who would never have considered stealing may now see petty shoplifting as a game. Thus the strength of this stage of moral reasoning—desire for approval—is also its weakness.

To a degree this is good because it is more mature than the reward-punishment orientation of childhood. On the other hand, the young adolescent can be tyrannized by the judgements of others. Eventually, he or she will move on to more internal, more personal judgements of what is "right," but this is a necessary middle step.

UNDERSTANDING FAMILIES WITH YOUNG ADOLESCENTS

SEEKING INDEPENDENCE

Teenagers want and need to take charge of their own lives, to make their own decisions, to choose their own friends, to plan their own activities, to think their own thoughts and to dream their own dreams. The relationship between parent and child inevitably changes as the adolescent becomes less an extension of his family and more an individual. Giving up childish images of a mother or father as all-knowing and all-powerful, for a more realistic (and critical) appraisal of parents as *people*, is part of this process. Young adolescents may not know who they are, but they do know they are more than a parent's son or daughter. The family used to be the center of their emotional life; now peers and other adults are also important to their feelings of self-worth and self-esteem, sometimes more so. Not surprisingly, both adolescents and their parents may feel ambivalent about these changes.

Growth toward independence is easy to mistake for rebellion. Rather suddenly, adolescents may begin questioning values, challenging opinions, debating the rules and distancing themselves from you. At the same time, they may treat their friends as the ultimate authority on everything from hair styles to global politics. As painful as it may be, however, this doesn't mean they are breaking away from their family and completely rejecting their upbringing. To some degree, all adolescents need to dissociate from their family and reject their image of them to become their own person.

The first steps toward independence are almost always taken at home. Because the adolescent knows (at least unconsciously) that home is a safe testing ground, where he is loved and mistakes will not be too costly, it is here that he (or she) will flex his (or her) muscles and test the rules.

What this means in day-to-day terms is that differences in opinion and approach, and confrontations tend to increase in early adolescence. Young adolescents may express their need to be independent of parental and adult authority by criticizing and quarreling or through silence and secrecy. This may cause a period of disequilibrium in families as the different family members adjust to the new person in their midst. In most cases, fortunately, this is short-lived. While disagreements are normal and common during the "adjustment" stages, constant fighting and out-and-out rebellion (running away, using drugs, truancy or delinquency) are *not*. Such behavior is a sign that the adolescent is having trouble establishing independence and/or that parents are exercising too much or too little control.

Adolescence is the first time that young people are able to think—and worry—about what is happening to them. In the words of one writer, "Worry is the result of our knowing there is a future. When we think about that future and see that it might be uncomfortable, unpleasant or dangerous in some way, we worry." Small children don't think that far ahead; adolescents do.

Self-esteem tends to decline temporarily in early adolescence: 10- to 13-year-olds are much more likely than younger children to feel unhappy about their looks, unsure of their abilities or worried about their popularity. At the same time, self-consciousness increases. Young adolescents wonder, *"Can I do it?"*, *"Will I look stupid?"*, *"Will I make friends?"*, *"What will they think of me?"*

Vulnerability can spring from doubts about one's popularity, comfort in relating with peers of the same or opposite sex, or ability to meet others' expectations regarding academics, athletics or both.

That's the bad news. The good news is that this period of increased vulnerability is temporary. By ninth grade, self-esteem has begun to stabilize; in middle and late adolescence, feelings of self-worth usually increase. In other words, vulnerability does not entirely pervade adolescence.

THE SOCIAL WORLD OF THE YOUNG ADOLESCENT

In childhood, peer groups are organized and supervised by adults. Opportunities to socialize depend on who lives near whom, who is in your Cub Scout pack or Little League team and whose parents are willing to host the pajama party. In adolescence, though, peer groups take on a life of their own.

Friends and peers become very important during the young adolescent years. Young adolescents want to do things as a group and to be with their friends; when that is not possible, the telephone is the next best thing! Peer relationships are crucial for healthy development. Through their friends, adolescents begin to learn to develop and maintain close, mutually supportive relationships with people their own age. Peers can press each other toward growth and responsibility or toward deviance, depending on their choice of friends. Being able to relate to peers and fit into a peer group is a necessary stage in adolescent development and, contrary to popular belief, parents can play an important role in providing support and encouragement for their young adolescents in developing *positive* relationships.

Peer groups serve a purpose. At a stage when adolescents are wondering, "Who will I become?", the group provides an answer: "A member of The Group." What should I wear? Should I try out for the team? Study all night? Be nice to this person? Joke with those boys? The group provides answers. Because an individual adolescent believes that everyone is constantly watching his or her appearance and every act, it is very painful to be "different." To compensate for this, younger adolescents try to look and act like their friends in order not to stand out. Having just the right jeans or tennis shoes is one way to express this need to fit in.

PEER PRESSURE

Although it is true that peers become more influential, parents and families still remain important in setting values and giving affection. In fact, adolescents agree with and follow their parents' advice more often than many would like to admit. As a general rule, adolescents seem to accept their parents' views on "big issues," such as moral and religious values, but follow their peers on matters of style: in music, clothes, hair, neatness and so on. They listen to their parents more than their peers on questions relating to their future (college and career choices) but to their peers more than their parents on issues that affect their current social life (choice of friends and activities).

When parents and adolescents do argue about controversial issues such as sex and drugs, the differences between them are often a matter of degree. For example, parents may believe that a couple should only have sex if they are married; their adolescent may feel that a couple should only have sex if they are planning to get married. Their arguments may be heated, but in terms of national norms, both generations are on the conservative or traditional side. Adolescents are most likely to turn to their peers when they believe, rightly or wrongly, that their parents have little experience or expertise about something (for example, drugs) or when their parents seem unable or unwilling to advise them (for example, about sex).

If you are worried about peer pressure, remember that adolescents who have warm, affectionate relationships with their parents—adolescents who like their parents and whose parents like them and *show it*—are less likely to agree to something they don't want to do than are adolescents whose relationships with their parents are cool and distant. One reason is that they tend to have more self-esteem and self-esteem increases self-confidence and assertiveness. Another is that they tend to choose friends whom their parents like, and who probably believe in staying out of trouble, doing well in school and behaving responsibly.

CHANGES IN FAMILY RELATIONSHIPS

While we are all aware of the important and substantive changes occurring in the lives of young adolescents, it is extremely important to keep in mind that adolescence is a period of change and reorganization in family relationships as well. Our approach to the family will look at the family as a whole to see how the changes in adolescents and in their parents affects the entire system of relationships which creates the family.

The concerns and issues characteristic of families at adolescence arise not just because of the changing needs and concerns of the young person, but also because of changes in their parents and in the needs and functions of the family as a unit. Consequently, we must take into account not only characteristics of the developing young person but those of the adolescent's parents and families as well.

In general, the critical developmental periods for the family are those times characterized by fundamental, rapid and/or dramatic change in one of the family members. Such periods are especially disquieting for the family because its members' competencies and concerns are changing, and the family must adapt to them. When a number of its individual members are changing simultaneously, the family experiences periods of even greater disequilibrium. Adolescence, because it is a time of profound change in the young adolescent *and* in the parents, is one such critical period. And it is because the family system must adapt to changes both in the adolescent and in the parents that this time is particularly trying for some families.

These changes in the family system during adolescence bring about periods of disequilibrium or imbalance—times when an individual member has changed but the system has not yet fully adapted by altering relationships. A healthy family system will adapt to this new stage by meeting the challenge and bringing about balance or equilibrium. These changes occur gradually, in a somewhat disorganized way, as individuals try on new roles and experiment with new ways of relating to each other.

Adjustments must take place in families with young adolescents to take into account their new needs and abilities and the concerns of the family members. Difficulties that occur during adolescence often result from an inability on the part of family members to acknowledge these changes, to change their expectations and to find new ways to communicate with each other.

Several examples may illustrate the changes in family relationships during early adolescence. Our examples will look at the impact of new thinking abilities, sexual growth and the struggle of freedom and limits.

First, the adolescent's new reasoning abilities make it exceedingly difficult for a parent to exercise previously unquestioned authority. Prior to adolescence, it is relatively simple for a parent to lay down a set of rules and insist that children abide by them. In adolescence, however, the child begins to develop intellectual abilities which may be equal to those of adults. The young person may feel entitled to have more say in family decision-making and may no longer accept a parent's word as final.

The emergence of independent behavior may be construed by parents as adolescent rebelliousness when, in fact, the behavior is likely to have little to do with the adolescent's feelings toward the parents and more to do with a desire to exercise new intellectual skills. A healthy family adjusts by including the adolescent in family discussions on a more adult level.

As young adolescents use new thinking skills and develop an interest in the world around them, they may bring home new ideas and attitudes that encourage change in other family members. Sometimes these new ideas may be welcomed like a breath of fresh air, and other times, they may create conflict within the family.

Second, coping with the physical and sexual changes of young adolescents is a major task for all family members. It is not uncommon for family members to experience a wide range of feelings as they adjust to a son, daughter or sibling whose body is maturing quickly. As parents, our own experience with sexual development and relationships will influence the way in which we are able to respond to and support our young adolescents as they go through puberty and begin to explore who they are sexually.

It is not uncommon for changes in young adolescents to stir up issues that we as parents have yet to resolve in our own lives. A young adolescent daughter's ideas about what roles women should play, for instance, can rekindle a mother's desires for personal growth and understanding, and perhaps lead her to seek the support of other women. In responding to her daughter's sexual growth, a mother may get in touch with her own needs for growth and change.

Third, it can be difficult to find the right balance of freedom and limits that is so necessary for young adolescents, and the resulting tug-of-war can be stressful for everyone.

Adolescents may feel strong and independent one minute and childlike the next, as they grow toward adulthood. Because of this, they may vacillate about many things, many times a day. They can see you (as a parent) as being wonderful one minute and positively awful the next; one day your ideas make sense but the next you know nothing.

Young teenagers can also exhibit wide swings in mood, degree of responsibility and attitude toward family values, rules and traditions as they try to assert their independence and separateness. Adolescents will often test, attack or discard a parental value as a way of establishing their own values and identity. When this happens it is very important for parents to stand firm and state clearly what expectations they have about the adolescent's behavior while living in their home.

It is crucial that parents set clear limits for their young adolescent children. Because it is during this time that young people make their first major thrust to separate from their family, it is important that they have something to break away *from*. If parents keep changing their values, rules and positions on issues because of resistance from their adolescent, they will not be helping their child find his own value system but just confusing him. This does not mean, however, that rules should be rigid, because then you risk cutting off communication with your teenagers. A firm yet flexible position is more difficult to maintain because it calls for more judgment. It is fine to compromise and negotiate on certain reasonable issues; that is where flexibility enters.

Although the skills needed for creative discipline with adolescents are basically the same for all families, some families face special challenges. Single parents who carry the responsibility for discipline alone can find it difficult, at times, to balance the needs for supporting and providing structure for their young adolescents. In blended families, and especially new ones with "instant" adolescents, young people may reject discipline attempts by a new step parent. In any family, children may attempt to play off one parent against the other. While parents may not always agree on all issues, discipline is easiest when parents, family members and friends support one another in this crucial task.

GROWING IN FAITH

Many young adolescents derive their faith, beliefs and values mainly from parents and family through earlier experiences and parent role modeling. This style of faith can be called *experienced faith*. Other young adolescents are beginning to step beyond *experienced* faith to *conventional faith*. In conventional faith a person's beliefs and values become more rooted in the convictions and commitments proclaimed and lived out by the larger faith community. Conventional faith builds upon and expands experienced faith.

Adolescents struggle to answer the twin questions of "Who am I?" and "What will I become?" In search of an answer to these questions the adolescent tries on different roles to see how well they fit, how comfortable they are, how much security they bring. They learn who and whose they are by experiencing a sense belonging and by active involvement in the life of the faith community. In the process, they slowly take to themselves the beliefs, value and attitudes of the people they have come to know and trust in the faith community. These roles are worn by adults who both prove themselves trustworthy and lovable to the adolescent and at the same time confirm that he or she is a trustworthy and lovable person. The search for identity focuses upon models who exemplify faith in the form of fidelity, a trusting commitment of one person for another.

For *conventional faith* to blossom in the lives of young adolescents several elements are important. Among these are involvement in community, a participation in family and community life, realistic role models of faith, occasions to share faith stories, experiences of challenge and conflict and an exploration of the roots of the Christian life in Scripture and theology.

Involvement in programs of service to others during early adolescence can be an important means of developing a critical perspective and sense of justice. Even the dynamic of friendship can be extended across racial, religious and national boundaries to include people in groups and countries different than one's own. This exposure to other cultures, life situations and values can expand young people's sense of self and help them see how they "fit" in the faith community.

SUMMARY

Some parents of young adolescents may feel a need to evaluate their relationships and commitments or re-focus their marriage relationship as they struggle through the changes of the teenage years. During the last several years, both my husband and I have spent time learning about some of the relationship patterns in the families in which we grew up and how these patterns play themselves out in our present family. What we have experienced and learned has led us to make changes in our own lives, in our marriage and in our parenting. We have had to renegotiate roles and boundaries with one another, with extended family and with our children. At times, it has been hard work, but we are learning to be more flexible as a family and to respect one another's differences. In the process of growing and changing myself, I am learning to be more understanding and supportive of the growth and change that our young adolescent daughter is experiencing.

Families with young adolescents often feel the need to make changes in the ways they relate to one another, in the way the family is structured, and to renegotiate roles as they adjust to the growth of young adolescents and other family members. Most families, after a certain amount of confusion and disruption, are able to change the rules and limits and reorganize themselves. The normal stress and tension caused by changes in young adolescents can be increased when parents, grandparents or other family members also feel the need to make changes. Flexibility may be the key to success for families at the young adolescent stage of the family life cycle.

Learning to adapt is a gradual process; do not expect overnight miracles. Although early adolescence may not be an easy time for the family—no period during which family members are changing so rapidly is—it is a time of important family development and growth. All families must make the shift from relationships suited to parent and child to those appropriate for parent and young adult. In the long run, the emergence of this new relationship is more satisfying to both parents and young adolescents.

3

PARENTING SKILLS FOR FAITH GROWTH

Being a good parent does not come naturally or automatically to most people. It often involves learning a "new language" and "unlearning" some of the patterns and behaviors that we learned from being parented ourselves. In this chapter, we will look at some parenting skills that can help in building close relationships with your young adolescent and creating a family environment in which faith sharing can take place.

STRENGTHENING THE RELATIONSHIP BETWEEN PARENT AND YOUTH

During adolescence the parenting role begins to shift in major ways. As young people begin to take more personal responsibility for their own lives and grow increasingly independent, parents are faced with the task of restructuring their relationships with their young adolescents. Part of that restructuring involves laying the foundation for a new adult-to-adult relationship with them that will endure into the future. Working to build a new, adult relationship with your young adolescent does not mean you have to set aside your parenting responsibilities, but it can help you look on those responsibilities in a new way. As the new relationship grows, your influence also grows, based not on control but on mutual respect. The following, simple approaches can be helpful in creating a new, strong relationship with your young adolescent:

- Make time to talk with and listen to each other.
- Do things together that feel good and allow the time needed to build a new relationship.
- Pay attention to how well the two of you are getting along, ironing out problems together as they arise.
- Make sure you are both getting your needs met, while remaining sensitive to your teen's needs.

The process is simple enough. Relate to your young adolescent as you would relate to any good friend. Stay with the relationship and watch it grow.

PARENT-CHILD COMMUNICATION

Even when parents and adolescents consciously make time for one another, they sometimes find it difficult to connect with each other's thoughts and feelings. New experiences and relationships demand new ways of communicating. Learning new approaches to communication can be an important step in helping the relationships with your young adolescent to grow and flourish.

Roadblocks to Healthy Communication

A first step in establishing good communication within the family is reducing communication blocks. Without realizing it, sometimes we speak to our young adolescents in ways that are all but guaranteed to cut off communication. Some of the most common obstacles to communication are:

- *Criticism and ridicule.* Negative evaluations are communication-killers. Labeling, personal attacks, sarcasm and put-downs all fall into this category. Parents sometimes feel that if they do not criticize their young adolescent, he or she will never learn. Criticism doesn't make young people want to change; it makes them defensive.

- *Giving too many orders or too much advice.* Commands, threats and sermons (statements that begin with "you should/should not") are obvious turn-offs, especially to young adolescents who are struggling for autonomy. So is unsolicited advice.

- *Treating your young adolescent's problems lightly.* When parents attempt to reassure their young adolescent ("Cheer up...", "Don't worry..."), or divert their attention ("You think you have it tough, when I was your age..."), they may have the best of intentions, but the underlying message is that the adolescent's worries are trivial.

Instead of promoting communication, put-downs, orders and casual reassurance will trigger defensiveness, resistance and resentment, and undermine our young adolescent's self-esteem.

It is important for us as parents to remember that young adolescents are still in the process of developing their skills for communication. Limited verbal skills and difficulty in describing feelings and emotions will influence how a young adolescent is able to communicate with a parent. In addition, young adolescents are often very sensitive to negative feedback and criticism as they try to understand and accept the enormous physical, emotional and cognitive changes that are occurring within them. As young adolescents mature, they naturally grow in their desire to make personal decisions and may resist efforts by parents to assert our authority.

Effective Communication

There are so many wonderful books available to help parents improve their skills for parenting. Below are some suggestions which have been particularly helpful in my own experience of parenting a young adolescent.

Recognize and accept where young adolescents are developmentally.
It is natural for young adolescents to be pre-occupied with themselves as they experience tremendous amounts of change. Be sensitive and very careful about giving negative feedback. Simply asking a "feeling" question, such as "How do you feel about. . .?" may open new dimensions in conversations. Engaging one's young adolescent in conversation requires patience, time and the choice of a non-threatening situation.

Take time to establish relationships and do things together.
Parents often misinterpret their young adolescent's heightened interest in friends as disinterest in the family. In fact, studies show that most young adolescents would like to spend *more*, not less, time with their parents than they do now. Time together can mean going to a special event or sharing an activity you both enjoy as a way to get to know the person your young adolescent is becoming.

Learn to listen with your heart.
Listening with the heart is a basic requirement for understanding one's young adolescent and other members of our family. It is the only way by which we can come to understand who another person really is. Listening is a vital aspect of parenting and family life. The essence of listening with our heart is to put our whole self into trying to hear what our

young adolescent is saying. It is a way of showing that we care enough to put our own agenda aside long enough to really focus on the other person. We sacrifice our time, convenience or our own ideas about how things should be to hear the feelings behind our young adolescent's words or behaviors.

Share appropriate thoughts and feelings.
Some parents find it hard to admit to their young adolescents that they have personal struggles and failures. Actually, when both parent and young adolescent are free to reveal their humanness and their capacity for failure and struggle, a mutual understanding and trust is built which can be an important part of parent-child communication. However, this kind of sharing is not the same as a parent treating a young person as an emotional equal and using her or him as a confidant in the absence of other adults. This is not appropriate sharing and can be very harmful to the young adolescent.

Focus on the concerns and interests of the young adolescent.
Young adolescents want to talk about issues that parents often wish they could discuss, namely, their worries. For parents, these concerns can provide openings to discuss numerous topics. Parents must be aware that young people often have neither the courage nor the know-how to initiate conversation about their worries. To young adolescents, personal problems are mountainous obstacles; they are afraid parents will consider these same problems as insignificant, and so the parents are never made aware of the worries and given a chance to help. Parents need to initiate conversations in these areas because young people are discussing these things with others, like their peers.

A general question or comment in any one of the following topic areas may become the occasion for a good conversation:

Family Matters. Young adolescents want to be in on decisions that affect the whole family (like moving and vacations) as well as decisions that affect them (like allowance, curfew, rules). If there is a problem in the family (money problems, job pressures, an impending divorce, a serious illness), they want to know about it.

Controversial Issues. Young adolescents are full of questions. Is it ever right to tell a lie? What does sex feel like? What do people mean when they say drugs make you high? What does "gay" mean? They wish their parents would talk with them about these controversial subjects instead of saying "You're too young" or "It's too complicated to explain."

Emotional Issues. Young adolescents would like to know how their parents really feel about things. And they would like their parents to tell them "I love you" more often than most do.

The Big Whys. Why do people go to war? Why does God let people go hungry? On the verge of philosophical thinking, young adolescents wish their parents would talk about the big questions.

The Future. Children want to know what it's like to be a teenager, and teenagers want to talk about their future—jobs, careers, technical school/college.

Current Affairs. Young adolescents are often more aware of, and concerned about, current events than parents realize. When something happens in the world or in their community, they want to talk about it.

Personal Interests. Young adolescents wish their parents would show more interest in them—in their sports, hobbies and friends. Often they worry about how they are doing in school, their looks or that a parent might die, as well as how they are being treated by friends and losing a best friend.

Parents Themselves. Young adolescents want to know more about what their parents were like at their age. They particularly like stories that reveal their parents' emotional side and human frailties.

Family History and Heritage. Part of learning more about ourselves is learning more about the families from which we came. Young adolescence is a wonderful time to pull out family albums and share family stories about aunts and uncles, grandparents and distant relatives. Along with the stories, family traditions and values can be passed on and ethnic/national celebrations endowed with new meaning. Rooting young adolescents firmly in their past can provide them with the balance they need to step out on their own.

COLLABORATIVE PROBLEM-SOLVING

Occasional conflict and disagreement are normal occurrences in families with young adolescents. Effective communication and a collaborative approach to problem-solving provide an effective means of handling the changes and disruptions that occur regularly in family life.

Sometimes parents attempt to resolve conflicts with their adolescents by cracking down, giving in, avoiding the problem and compromise. Although each of these strategies has its uses, each also has its drawbacks. The problem with all these responses is that they don't resolve the conflict. Moreover, with each of these strategies somebody loses. Collaborative problem-solving provides an alternative to these no-win approaches.

The goal of collaborative problem-solving is to find a win/win solution that satisfies everyone. This approach takes time and energy. It requires the unhappy family members to confront one another, which isn't always pleasant. But in most cases it minimizes hostility and hurt feelings and maximizes the chances that you will truly resolve the issue.

There are six basic steps to collaborative problem-solving. The formula may seem awkward at first, but after you've used it several times it will become more natural. This approach works best if you choose a time and place when both you and your young adolescent will not be distracted, limit the discussion to a specific issue, and secure in advance your son or daughter's agreement to try to work out a solution.

Step 1. Establish ground rules. The ground rules for conflict resolution are essentially the rules of a fair fight.

Each party agrees to treat the other party with respect—no name-calling, sarcasm or put-downs—and to listen to the other person's point of view. Parents can set the stage by stating at the beginning their desire to be fair.

Step 2. Reach mutual understanding. The next step is to take turns being understood. This means that each of you will have the opportunity to say what you think the real problem is and how you feel about it. It's important that you get it off your chest. But it's also important to avoid loaded words and phrases, accusations and evaluations, and to focus on the issue, not on personalities. Each of you also has the right to be understood. This is where reflective listening enters. When you've described the problem as you see it, let the adolescent speak her piece. Then rephrase the adolescent's point of view and ask her to restate yours, so that you are sure you understand one another.

Step 3. Brainstorm. The next step is for each of you to think of as many solutions to the problem as you can. The goal of brainstorming is quantity, not quality. At this stage, no idea should be rejected because it's crazy, or too expensive, or one of you thinks it is dumb. Zany ideas can reduce tension and keep creative juices flowing. Set a time limit (five minute should be enough) and write down everything you can think of.

Step 4. Agree to one or more solutions. The best way to go about this is for each of you to select the options you like best. (Don't discuss each and every option; this can lead to endless, often fruitless, debate.) Then see where your interests coincide. Have you chosen any of the same options? Some give and take or negotiation will be necessary at this stage, and you need to think through the practical considerations. But neither of you should agree to something you still find unacceptable.

Step 5. Write down your agreement. This may sound excessively formal, but memory can be faulty. If either of you thinks the other has broken the agreement, you can refer to your contract.

Step 6. Set a time for a follow-up discussion to evaluate your progress. This is as important as the first five steps. One of you might not live up to the agreement, or the solution might not be as elegant as you thought, and you will have to work out the bugs.

This six-step formula can be applied to a variety of situations, from arguments over the adolescent's curfew to decisions about family vacations. In some cases you won't be able to reach an agreement. When it comes to health and safety, parents may have to make a unilateral decision. But adolescents are far more likely to go along with you when they participate in the decision-making process and when they see that you are taking their needs and desires seriously.

POSITIVE DISCIPLINE

As our children have grown, I have found that I have needed to learn new and different ways of parenting. These shifts in how we deal with young adolescents are, in effect, a recognition and affirmation of the growth that is taking place in their lives. The following guidelines have helped me to interact more positively with our children even in the difficult area of discipline.

An adolescent needs clear, firmly established rules.
This means a clear definition of acceptable and unacceptable conduct as well as a clear statement of consequences if the rule is broken. What causes young adolescents to rebel is not the assertion of authority but the arbitrary use of power, with little explanation of the rules and no involvement in decision-making. When parents show respect for their young adolescent's point of view, are willing to discuss rules and regulations and explain why they have to insist on this or forbid that, the young adolescent is much less likely to rebel. Young people may not always like your final decision, but most likely they will at least see you as fair. Involving the adolescent in decisions doesn't mean that you are giving up your authority. It means acknowledging that your child is growing

up and has the right to participate in decisions that affect his or her life.

Parents need to be flexible when the situation warrants it.
Issues relating to household responsibilities and personal behavior should be worked out by adolescents and parents together, taking into account the needs and desires of both. For example, how the adolescent keeps her room, how she dresses, when she does her homework, how much time she spends on the phone should be negotiable. None of these are matters of life and death. But unless you and the adolescent reach an understanding, you may find yourself constantly quarreling.

There are times when you have to draw the line.
Parents and adolescents should be clear about which family rules are negotiable and which are not. Issues that relate to physical and emotional safety and to deeply held family values fall into the category of non-negotiable rules. Adolescents may challenge these rules, but they are much more likely to comply with them if you limit non-negotiable rules to issues that really matter and you have solid, logical reasons for these rules.

Consistency in defining and applying discipline is essential.

- *Consistent in enforcement.* Don't enforce a rule one time but let it slide the next time because you're tired or you want to avoid a confrontation. When you're not consistent, the adolescent will see any discipline as arbitrary.

- *Consistent with your spouse.* If you and your partner disagree about what you should expect from the adolescent, work out your differences in private and present a united front to the child. Don't let the adolescent play one of you against the other.

- *Consistent with your values and beliefs.* If you stress the importance of honesty, don't blow up when your son is being honest and tells you that he cut school for three days in a row. Sit down and talk about why he cut school and what the two of you can do to solve the problem. Also take time to acknowledge and explain social and behavioral expectations that derive from your family's cultural heritage.

- *Consistent in the face of pressure from your child.* All adolescents test the limits on occasion. They may complain that everybody else's parents are more liberal, accuse you of picking on them and whine and sulk when you don't give in. Sometimes parents do give in because consciously or unconsciously, they are afraid their adolescent won't like them if they stick to their principles. But what adolescents don't like is the arbitrary use of power. Don't be afraid to be unpopular for a day or two.

Balancing consistency and flexibility in household rules and expectations can be particularly challenging in blended families or in situations where young adolescents move regularly between the homes of separated or divorced parents. Whatever the family structure, mutual respect, support and communication are needed between all parents united in the task of parenting an adolescent.

Disciplining must be a private affair. To be humiliated or embarrassed in front of friends or in a public place touches one of the most sensitive spots for an adolescent, namely, concern about the opinion of others, especially peers.

Conflict can be handled in a positive way. It is easy for parents to withdraw or react angrily when a teenager espouses a value different from that of the parent, but parents cannot afford to allow communication to break off in such situations. It is important to state clearly to each other what has been the cause of irritation and to try to work for a solution. The use of sarcasm or "rubbing it in" brings negative results.

PARENTING AND ENCOURAGEMENT

One of the key roles of parents is to encourage and enable the growth of their children. Parenting by encouraging builds self-esteem through focusing attention on young people's resources. An encouraging parent looks for the positive sides of his or her young adolescent's traits. Encouraging parents support their young adolescents' efforts to pursue their own goals, provided, of course, that the goals are reasonable and socially acceptable. Unlike praise, which rewards achievement and can foster competition or fear of failure, encouragement rewards effort and improvement, fostering cooperation and confidence. Consider the following strategies for encouraging the growth of adolescents in your family:

- Have positive expectations about what they can do and be.
- Emphasize the process (of living and learning), not just the product.
- Give them responsibility.
- Show appreciation for their contributions at home.
- Ask for their opinions and suggestions.
- Encourage their participation in decision making.
- Show confidence in their judgement.
- Respect their attempts.
- Accept their mistakes.
- Develop alternative ways of viewing situations.

COMMUNICATING WITH YOUR YOUNG ADOLESCENT ABOUT FAITH

As you spend time with your young adolescent and talk together about the people and events important in his life, you will be presented with numerous "teachable moments" where faith issues can naturally be raised. However, in order to be able to communicate with our young adolescents about our own values and beliefs from a faith perspective, we must first have wrestled with these ourselves.

What is going on in our own relationship with God and how does this influence our day-to-day life? It takes time and regular attention to our own spiritual growth to be able to understand and articulate how God is acting in our lives as adults. Giving time to reading and study on various issues can help us to articulate our values and beliefs in the light of faith to our children. It is difficult for parents to help young adolescents verbalize their beliefs and values, when we, as parents, haven't gone through the same process ourselves beforehand. Sharing our faith with young adolescents can be done in a variety of ways. Some approaches to faith sharing with young adolescents that have proved helpful to us follow.

SHARING FAITH IN THE NATURAL FLOW OF HOME LIFE

For many families, faith is connected to daily living and the ordinary routines of life. In fact, the primary expression of faith for the healthy family is in daily life. It is here that children and young adolescents learn about how to *live* faith and apply Christian values to everyday situations.

So many things in our lives can provide opportunities for us to share faith as families. In our family, the day-to-day interaction with our young adolescents provides ample opportunities to learn about respecting others accepting people who are different, saying "I'm sorry", sharing our time and talents with others, and making decisions about how to spend time and money (both of which seem limited some days). Learning to laugh together at the comic side of frustrating or hurtful situations and enjoying the beauty of nature during a family fishing trip can be other examples of sharing faith. We have the potential for discovering God at work in our personal lives and in our family life through the variety of life situations that we experience. These can become faith-sharing opportunities when we introduce our religious values into a discussion or decision, when we use our religious faith to evaluate and judge situations, when we give thanks for the many gifts God gives us, when we pray for guidance, when we celebrate forgiveness and reconciliation. The important thing as parents is to learn to be more *intentional* about finding ways to share faith with our children.

Encouraging our children to pray spontaneously is also important. Young adolescents can learn to bring their prayers of thanksgiving, personal problems and prayers for specific people and situations to God during times of family prayer and on their own. In our family, we include times for spontaneous prayer before meals and at bedtime.

SHARING STORIES OF FAITH

As important as faith may be, it still isn't a normal topic of dinner conversation in most families with young adolescents. Usually young people (and their parents) need a bit of assistance and structure in order to move faith to the forefront in family discussions. This activity takes a story sharing approach to discussing faith. It helps young people and their parents articulate why faith is important to them and how they find it in the ordinary experiences of their life. The process is a simple one that lends itself to use throughout the year.

Reflect: Use any or all of the following open-ended sentences as a starting point for a family discussion on faith. Choose the questions together. Give family members some quiet time to reflect on or write out their responses before moving to discussion.

- Something that is really different about Catholicism today, compared to 20 years ago is....
- In my experience as a teenager, attending Mass on Sunday.....
- A person who has really influenced my faith life..... She or he influenced me by.....
- As a child, I was taught to pray..... Now I pray.....
- Something I love about being part of the Church.....
- A difficulty I have with the Church.....
- A time in my life when I really needed God was.....

- When I think about Jesus.....
- I believe faith is important because.....

Share: Invite family members to share their reflections. Some may find it difficult to share aloud the first time or two, so patience is essential. Just talking about faith together reflects its importance in your life and offers family members a chance to rethink how they see or experience faith.

A few hints on dialoguing about faith with adolescents:

- Allow and encourage young people to be honest with themselves and with you about their faith journey. For some young people faith is a certainty. For others it is a real struggle. Both faith stances can be very real. Both need to be respected.

- For many young people faith is most tangible when seen through the perspective of personal relationships and/or values. Raising the issue of who and what they believe in, and why, can be a fruitful starting point for discussions of faith.

- Be flexible in your conversations about faith. Discussing issues and questions of immediate concern to young people, even when the issues do not appear to be explicitly religious, can be a prelude to an encounter with the deeper questions of personal faith.

Pray: Close your sharing of faith stories with a simple, spontaneous prayer, or ask a family member in advance to come prepared with a brief closing prayer.

SHARING FAITH THROUGH CULTURE AND FAMILY HERITAGE

Ethnic and national culture can have a profound effect on how families with young adolescents share faith. The unique histories and faith experiences of different cultures have given rise to unique religious perspectives, traditions and practices. Some of these differences become apparent in the diverse ways that families celebrate the church seasons of Advent or Lent or in how they celebrate milestone events in family life like special birthdays, graduations or weddings. Others are revealed through the simple ways that families live out their faith on day-to-day basis. These different approaches to faith are sure to catch the eye of young adolescents and can provide a unique opportunity for sharing faith as family. Help your young adolescent to see these differences as special gifts that celebrate past connections and that help make God's presence real for your family today. As mentioned earlier, faith for young adolescents is about belonging and learning the faith values of the community. Sharing your family's culture and heritage with young adolescents can help them feel more a part of the family and draw the connection between family and faith life.

SHARING FAITH THROUGH A DIALOGUE ABOUT VALUES

Young adolescents need to be able to ask questions and venture opinions as they learn about the values, beliefs and practices of family and communal faith. Ideally, there are no "unaskable" questions about faith. Opportunities to question, make distinctions and examine beliefs gives young adolescents a chance to "test out" their faith. When young adolescents sense that we as parents are open to discussions that allow them to explore and test out ideas, they are more likely to come to us.

In the past months, our 11-year-old daughter has asked me at different times about my opinions on issues such as abortion, war and homosexuality. Beth usually begins by citing something that she has seen or heard and then asks what I think. After making sure that I understood her question, I shared with her some of my own values and beliefs and how my faith has helped me to form them. I could see the wheels turn as she compared what I was saying to what she had heard. I know that Beth needs time to "try on" different opinions, values and beliefs as a way of coming to a faith that is her own—a faith that will speak to the complexity of life around her. Hopefully, my husband and I can be positive influences for her in that process.

SHARING FAITH DURING STRUCTURED TIMES OF FAMILY WORSHIP

These structured times may be some form of family "worship," ritual or family devotion. Some parents may have memories of devotions or family prayer when they were younger that they want to pass on to their children.

Family worship or ritual may take many forms, yet what is important is that families have the opportunity to *experience* faith together. Young adolescents learn what faith means to them by observing and participating in how their parents and the Christian community celebrate faith. This is how faith becomes real for them.

Celebrating ritual as families may happen around certain liturgical seasons, holidays, birthdays, graduations or other special occasions. These types of occasions attest to the fact that celebrations of life for the Christian family are linked with belief and faith.

SHARING FAITH BY WORKING FOR JUSTICE AND SERVING OTHERS

As we grow in our faith, we become more aware of how central God's justice was to Jesus' life and ministry. As Catholic Christians, working for justice and peace is at the heart of our faith. As parents of young adolescents, this dimension of faith, as with other dimensions we have previously discussed, can be incorporated into our parenting and family lifestyles in a variety of ways. Families with young adolescents can put their faith into practice by:

- promoting self-esteem, communication, and positive ways to resolve conflict within the family;
- educating family members about social issues;

- encouraging cooperation and interdependence at home and in interaction with others;
- caring for the earth and its resources;
- sharing family time, talents and possessions with people in need;
- working to create an environment at home that is free of physical and emotional violence which can include how we discipline our young adolescents, how spouses and other adults express anger and resolve conflict, how TV shows, movies, video games, sports and other forms of entertainment are chosen and shared;
- standing in opposition to the violence that permeates our culture and world;
- living simply and taking good care of personal and family possessions;
- praying as a family for those in need;
- participating in a service project as a family.

I have found a great deal of diversity in how families with young adolescents seek to put the social teachings of the Catholic Church into practice. A number of families that I know have started making a real effort to recycle, often with their young adolescents leading the way in this effort. As they connect this effort to God's call to care for the earth and its resources, families put their faith into practice.

In my family, my husband and I have tried to encourage the idea that we belong to one global family in various ways. For example, in our living room, we have a picture of the earth as it was taken from space during one of the landings on the moon. During the past two years, we have had a lot of conversations in our family about what has been happening in the world—in Africa, China, Europe and the Commonwealth of Independent States. Several years ago, I had the opportunity to be involved in a project in which I learned much more about what the Church is doing to work for justice in Latin America. Very often, our faith provides a very different perspective of what is happening in the world than does the 6:00 PM news. We want to encourage our young adolescents to ask questions and to seek truth. We want them to live together in peace with people of different skin colors, different beliefs, different races, different sexes.

Actions of direct service are a logical starting point for families with young adolescents. Young adolescents easily connect with direct service and the needs that prompt it. Being involved with service projects allows them to give of themselves and to see the results of their efforts. As parents, it is important to assist young adolescents in connecting acts of service to others with our faith. Young adolescents need to know that they are important and that God can use them right now.

One challenge for families is to try to make helping actions as empowering as possible for the people who are being helped. Many young adolescents will have no trouble in understanding the importance of people being able to direct their own lives and being able to participate in the decisions that affect their lives. In addition, it is important to assist our young adolescents in understanding the need to change those situations that make victims in the first place. Participating in the struggles for social change can be hope-giving for young adolescents if the issues are concrete enough or have a direct bearing on them.

NURTURING OUR OWN FAITH GROWTH AS ADULTS

Young adolescents sense when faith is important to their parents. The visible, consistent and joyful living of our own faith as parents can be a powerful influence in forming the faith of our young adolescents. Faith is probably "caught" more through our example than by anything we might say to our young adolescents.

In this society, where religion often seems the domain of women, the faith commitments of fathers are very important. Mothers are crucial for sharing and nurturing faith growth as we have always known. It is important that fathers also become mediators and nurturers of faith. The father is an important influence on whether that family system will have an overall sense of religious orientation and faith. In many families grandparents and relatives are also powerful influencers of the faith and values of adolescents.

How do we as parents nurture our own faith growth? Responses to this question might include regular reflection and prayer, Scripture, liturgy, spiritual direction, a support or prayer group, participation in a parish renewal program, attending workshops, reading, retreats, etc. However we do it, it is important that our young adolescents see us making efforts to nurture our own faith growth.

SUMMARY

Nurturing and empowering young adolescents and passing on faith are very important tasks. Few people come to the experience of parenthood fully equipped to handle all that they will encounter. Most often, parenting is a process learned along the way. How we image our role as parent will make a big difference in how we approach the tasks of parenting and family life.

4

STRATEGIES AND ACTIVITIES

A shared faith provides families with a common set of values and a purpose in today's world, and can be an important element in strengthening and promoting healthy family life. A family-shared faith can be a source of strength for young adolescents as they confront new experiences and challenges in their life. Faith can assist young adolescents in choosing values and behaviors which are both growthful and life-giving.

A shared faith can also be an important resource during times of change and stress in family life. It helps families maintain a sense of hope and gratefulness. It provides valuable perspective as family members make important decisions or go about the ordinary business of family life.

While parents may feel responsible for "sharing faith," it is important that they do so in positive and meaningful ways that recognize the young adolescent's need to question. There are many possible approaches that families with young adolescents can take in their attempts to share faith together. Consider the following.

SHARING THE CATHOLIC FAITH STORY

Families play a key role in sharing the values and beliefs of the Catholic community. This is done when:

- all family members, especially adults, continue to grow in their own faith through reading, informal discussion or participation in parish or community educational programs and share their learnings with one another;
- families participate in intergenerational catechetical experiences, gathering with other families to learn, grow and live the Catholic faith;
- families make the connection between their life experiences and faith values, drawing on the rich resources of Scripture, Catholic Tradition and the faith traditions found in their ethnic heritage;
- families participate together in the sacramental preparation of individual family members;
- families recognize the impact of media and learn to evaluate media critically in light of the life-giving values of the Catholic Christian faith.

The following activities provide examples of how the Catholic faith story can be shared meaningfully by families with young adolescents.

STRATEGIES AND ACTIVITIES

ACTIVITY 1. VALUES WE WANT TO SHARE: A REFLECTION ACTIVITY FOR PARENTS

The Church reminds us repeatedly today that faith is more a lifestyle than a listing of beliefs. As you reflect on the faith you want to pass on to the young person(s) in your family, what values do you consider essential to a true, lived faith?

Reflect: Take a piece of paper and jot brief responses to the following questions:

- What faith values do I most want to share with my child(ren)?
- What am I doing now to help this value come to life for my family?

Share: Share your responses with your spouse and/or a friend who shares your concern for faith. See what is most similar or dissimilar in your responses to these questions.

Compare: Compare your listing of essential values with that offered below. The list highlights values promoted in recent pastoral letters authored by the U.S. Catholic bishops.

Reflect Again: Look back on the values you previously listed as essential to a lived faith. How might you change your listing in light of the sharing and comparing you have done as part of this activity? What new steps can you take to make these values come to life in your family?

FAITH VALUES WORTH SHARING

Human Dignity and Equality. We believe that women and men are created by God and uniquely fashioned in God's image. Each and every person is sacred. Christians are called to lead lives and assist in building structures that respect the dignity and worth of every person, regardless of race, ethnic origin, religion, economic class, sex, sexual orientation, age, or physical or psychological limitations.

Human Rights. We believe that all human beings are entitled to the minimum conditions necessary for healthy growth. Minimum human rights include sufficient life goods, availability of education and work, cultural acceptance, economic justice and the right to political participation.

Community, Interdependence and Love. We believe that we are called to love our neighbor as ourselves, that life is meant to be lived in community, in relationships with other people. We believe that all people and all the different parts of God's creation are linked together. We are one human family, diverse and unique, but connected. In community we learn who and whose we are, building up one another and contributing to God's Kingdom in love.

Stewardship. We believe that God has entrusted us with the responsibility of using the world's resources wisely. The resources of the world are entrusted to us by God so that the needs of *all* people may be met.

Justice and Peace. We believe that the essential human needs of all people can be met and that Christians are called to address the social problems and social policies which keep people poor and oppressed. We believe that people are called to live in harmony with each other and with creation, to realize greater cooperation among peoples. When the demands of justice are met, peace will be reality.

Compassion and Service. We believe that we are called like Jesus to have a special sensitivity to human suffering and fragility, to love and to serve others as Jesus did. To show compassion for those who society considers outcasts or worthless is to love as Jesus loved. Christians are called to serve those in need and to work for a world freed of poverty and oppression.

Relationships and Sexuality. We believe that the quality of our relationships depends on the values of commitment, faithfulness, honesty and concern for the other person. We believe that sexuality is a gift from God, an integral part of our personhood.

Learn More About It:

Betz, Margaret. *Making Life Choices: How Personal Decisions Shape Our World.* Mahwah, NJ: Paulist Press, 1992.

ACTIVITY 2. PRINCIPLES FOR DEVELOPING A HEALTHY, CHRISTIAN VIEW OF SEXUALITY

Growing toward maturity in sexuality is a lifelong process. Both parents and young adolescents continue to grow as sexual persons. Four elements (gender, sex roles, sexual expression, beliefs and values) work together to form our identity as sexual persons. Church teaching provides a guide for shaping personal values and behaviors in the important area of sexuality. This teaching is based on Jesus' message of love and promotes respect for all life. Consider the following principles:

Gender

■ *A Christian person sees sexuality as a gift created by God.* Sexuality is part of who we are as human beings. We do not need to feel embarrassed or ashamed of our sexuality.

■ *A Christian person respects his or her own body and the bodies of others.* Scripture tells us that our bodies are to be temples of God. As we mature, we learn about and become more comfortable with the body that God has given us. Eating healthy, exercising and staying away from harmful substances are ways to care for our body and say thank you to God for creating us. To respect the bodies of others is to acknowledge that God is present in every person.

Sex Roles

- *A Christian person recognizes and affirms the equality of males and females.* Scripture tells us God created us male and female, and God saw that it was good. We believe as Christians that male and female represent two ways of being in the world, complementing the gifts of each other. Any suggestion that persons of one sex are better or more gifted than the other is a misunderstanding of God's creative purposes. We can recognize differences in males and females without developing negative stereotypes.

Expression

- *A Christian person builds healthy relationships through the values of commitment, faithfulness, honesty and a concern for the other person.* Each of us builds relationships with many different people throughout our lives. The quality of our relationships depends on the values of commitment, faithfulness, honesty and concern for the other person. The challenge of building healthy relationships begins with our own family (though sometimes it feels like this is the most difficult place to begin) and then extends outward to others.

- *A Christian person believes that sexual intercourse is an expression of love reserved for those in the permanent, life-giving commitment of marriage.* Sexual intercourse, along with other acts of physical affection, is a special way in which a man and woman pledge themselves to one another and to all that their lives together will demand of them. This pledge requires a serious adult commitment. Sexual intercourse is also the expression of love that God has given man and woman to share in the creation of a new life. It is only within marriage that sexual intercourse can be a sign of committed love and be open to bringing forth new life. Only in this relationship does sexual intercourse find its full meaning.

- *A Christian person has the right to say no to and reject sexual activity for any reason.* Sexual activity is not the same as love. Sexual activity can be a loving expression of commitment, or it can be used as a means of force to violate a person's dignity and self worth. It is wrong to pressure another person with words or actions that do not respect his/her rights.

Values and Beliefs

- *A Christian person believes in a loving God who creates each person as a unique expression of love and calls us to care for and serve others.* We believe that all life and all people are a part of God's creation, and therefore, we must show respect for others through our words and actions.
- *A Christian person believes that the gift of human sexuality carries with it the responsibility to grow into the persons God created us to be.* This is a lifelong process of saying yes to the way God calls us to mature.
- *A Christian person does not see abortion as a solution to an unwanted pregnancy.* The Catholic Church teaches that human life is present from the moment of conception. All life is a precious gift from God. Regardless of the circumstances in which a child is conceived, the new life is no less a person and no less precious and deserves protection, care and respect.

CELEBRATING RITUALS AND PRAYING TOGETHER

Families provide a sense of rhythm and celebration to their faith life by celebrating unique family rituals and participating in the ritual life of the parish community. This is done when:

- families celebrate the many ways that the sacred is revealed in their shared life through home rituals focused on ordinary family events, important milestones in family life, liturgical seasons and appropriate civic holidays;
- families regularly participate in the Sunday Eucharistic assembly;

- families actively participate in parish rituals that support and complement their home rituals and celebrations;
- all family members actively participate in the preparation and celebration of the sacramental rites of passage of family members through in-home activities and participation in parish programs;
- families reclaim, affirm and celebrate their own ethnic rituals and traditions, and participate in cultural and ethnic celebrations offered by the parish community and the wider Church and civic community.

Families encourage the development of a family prayer life and involve family members in the prayer life of the parish community. This is done when:

- parents and adult family members continue to grow by devoting time and care to their relationship with God through spiritual development programs and resources;
- families develop a pattern of family prayer which nurtures faith and sustains the family during times of change or crisis;
- parents help their children to pray in age-appropriate ways;
- families join with others in the parish community for prayer and support;
- families draw upon their ethnic prayer traditions in creating their family prayer pattern and draw on the cultural and ethnic prayer traditions of the extended family, parish and wider church community;
- parents encourage participation of family members in age-specific spiritual development programs and prayer experiences/services and connect an individual's experience in these programs to the family's prayer life.

The following activities provide practical examples of how families can share together in ritual and prayer during the young adolescent years.

ACTIVITY 1. SUGGESTIONS FOR PLANNING PRAYER AS A FAMILY

Prayer is most meaningful in families when everyone is involved in planning for the prayer event. Regardless of age, everyone can play a role in planning for and celebrating family prayer. Working together on *how* you will pray helps guarantee that *what* you pray about is felt by all. Some simple suggestions.

1. Choose a prayer occasion or event you would like to celebrate together as a family.

2. Check this chapter and the prayer resources listed to see how others have structured rituals for the same occasion or event.

3. Decide on the elements that will be part of your prayer.

- spontaneous or structured prayers (e.g., opening prayer, litany, blessing, Apostles' Creed, Our Father)
- readings from Scripture, poetry or literature
- centerpiece and environment (e.g. banners, photos, table cloth, plants, Bible, crucifix, candle, bowl)
- music
- simple gestures or movement

3. Look at the talents you share as a family.

Some people are natural researchers, ready to see what everyone else has written, while others prefer to create from scratch. Some hate to sing or read while others love the limelight. Some jump instantly into arts and crafts while others never will. Go with the flow of your family talents and inclinations while planning. Plan your prayer to fit your family...not the other way around.

4. Distribute the tasks based on ability and willingness, involving everyone in at least one element of preparation.

5. When you're ready, celebrate your prayer as family.

NOTE: In many families anything done together once is already a tradition. Make a tradition of family prayer and watch the difference it makes in you!

ACTIVITY 2. CELEBRATING GOD'S FORGIVENESS AS A FAMILY

Differences regularly arise and get settled in the normal course of family life with young adolescents. The experience of oneness that follows upon reconciliation is worth celebrating. It offers family members a chance to reflect on the affection they have for one another and helps them get in touch with the great love that God has for all people. Use the following service or adapt it to your family situation.

Begin with Prayer

Place a crucifix in the center of your family table or wherever you gather most comfortably for prayer. Ask family members to think about what the cross means as one person begins the prayer with these words:

> God, our Father,
> we needed a home,
> and so you made this beautiful world.
> We needed warmth and light,
> and you hung the sun in the sky.
>
> We needed food,
> and you blessed the fields with rain.
> We needed someone to love and care for,
> and you gave us each other.
> And when we quarreled and forgot your goodness,
> you planted a sign of love and forgiveness
> for all the world to see.
> You sent your only Son to live and die for us.
> He stretched out his arms on the cross
> to show how you long to embrace us all.
> We remember the story of Jesus,
> the story of your love for us

STRATEGIES AND ACTIVITIES

and the love we can have for one another,
with joy and thanksgiving
today and every day of our lives. Amen.

Share a Bible Story

Read one of the many biblical stories of forgiveness or one of the following biblical accounts:

- Ezekiel 36:23–28 (God's promise to warm the hard hearts of his people)
- John 1:1-5, 10–12, 14, 16 (the poetic portion of the Gospel's Prologue)
- 1 Corinthians 1:18–25 (Paul's insistence that the cross alone reveals what God is like)

Talk about the story and how it relates to your family situation.

Offer Thanks

Offer thanks for forgiveness that graces your home by praying together Psalm 128 or Psalm 133. Or let everyone express the personal joy of reconciliation and offer thanks, like this:

"José and I found a way to resolve our differences. Thank you, Lord."

"Mom hugged me when I told her I was sorry, and I felt good again. Thank you, Lord."

Join hands and pray as God's family: "Our Father..."

Close with a Gesture

- Trace the sign of the cross on one another's forehead as a reminder that you are God's children in a special way because of your Baptism.
- Share a hug, kiss or handshake.
- Listen to or sing together a song that speaks of love or forgiveness.

(Adapted from "Celebrating God's Forgiveness" by Carol Luebering in *The Forgiving Family*. St. Anthony Messenger Press, 1983.)

ACTIVITY 3. MARTIN LUTHER KING DAY

Martin Luther King, Jr.'s birthday, observed nationally on the third Monday in January, is a special day when people throughout the United States remember his commitment to civil rights and the continuing need to work together to erase instances of prejudice, injustice and inequality. His birthday helps us recall our responsibility as Christians to create a world where everyone's dignity is respected and where all people have what they need to live full and healthy lives. As young adolescents struggle with the important issues of dignity and freedom, Martin Luther King's life can take on special meaning for them.

There are many ways to make Dr. King's birthday a special celebration in your family's life. The following ritual offers one approach:

Preparation

In advance of Martin Luther King, Jr.'s birthday, learn more about his life and the civil rights movement in the United States.

Celebration

- Share a brief justice reading from Scripture, for example, Isaiah 58: 1–11 or 1 John 4: 7–20.
- Take turns as a family reading aloud the following brief excerpts from King's "I Have a Dream" address, which envisions a world where justice and love extend to all people:

> *So I say to you my friends, that even though we must face the difficulties of today and tomorrow, I still have a dream. It is a dream deeply rooted in the American dream that one day this nation will rise up and live out the true*

STRATEGIES AND ACTIVITIES

meaning of its creed—we hold these truths to be self-evident, that all men are created equal.

I have a dream that one day on the red hills of Georgia, sons of former slaves and sons of former slave-owners will be able to sit down together at the table of brotherhood.

I have a dream my four little children will one day live in a nation where they will not be judged by the color of their skin but by the content of their character. I have a dream today!

I have a dream that one day, little black boys and black girls will be able to join hands with little white boys and white girls as sisters and brothers. I have a dream today.

I have a dream that one day every valley shall be exalted, every hill and mountain shall be made low, the rough places shall be made plain, and the crooked places shall be made straight and the glory of the Lord will be revealed and all flesh shall see it together.

This is our hope. This is the faith I go back to the South with. With this faith we will be able to hew out of the mountains of despair a stone of hope.

With this faith we will be able to transform the jangling discords of our nation into a beautiful symphony of brotherhood.

With this faith we will be able to work together, to pray together, to struggle together, to go to jail together, to stand up for freedom together, knowing that we will be free one day.

This will be the day when all of God's children will be able to sing with new meaning—"my country 'tis of thee; sweet land of liberty; of thee I sing; land where my fathers died, land of the pilgrim's pride, from every mountain side, let freedom ring."

And when we allow freedom to ring, when we let it ring from every village and hamlet, from every state and city, we will be able to speed up that day when all of God's children—black and white, Jews and Gentiles, Catholics and Protestants—will be able to join hands and to sing in the words of the Old Negro spiritual, "Free at last, free at last; thank God Almighty, we are free at last."

■ Share together briefly the dreams you have for your family, for the people of your country and for all the people of the world. Talk about what you can do together as a family to make these dreams more of a reality.

■ Follow your sharing with this prayer:

Lord our God,
see how oppression and violence are our sad inheritance,
one generation to the next.
We look for you where the lowly are raised up,
where the mighty are brought down.
We find you there in your servants,
and we give you thanks this day
for your preacher and witness, Martin Luther King, Jr.
Fill us with your spirit:
where our human community is divided by racism,
torn by repression,
saddened by fear and ignorance,
may we give ourselves to your work of healing.
Grant this through Christ our Lord.
Amen.

■ In closing, sing a simple protest song from the civil rights movement like "We Shall Overcome."

Option: In place of an in-home celebration, participate as a family in a community celebration of King's birthday. Check your newspaper for details on how groups in your community are celebrating the holiday.

ACTIVITY 4. STEPFAMILIES: STRENGTHENING TIES THROUGH PRAYER AND RITUAL

By establishing their own traditions and rituals, stepfamilies build family bonds and create a family identity of their own. Family traditions shared year after year build a sense of permanence and continuity for family members. They provide shared memories of enjoyable times spent together that can sustain family members through the periods of change and conflict that are part of life in all families.

If young adolescents divide their holiday time between two different homes or enter a blended family with established holiday traditions and rituals, it may be difficult to negotiate new and meaningful ways of celebrating the major holidays and holy days of the year. But that doesn't stop families from creating alternative celebrations or expanding their repertoire of family rituals.

Christmas spent with one parent (or set of parents) can be supplemented with a special "Little Christmas" celebration on the feast of the Epiphany, January 6—the twelfth day of Christmas celebrated with much fanfare and joy in the countries of Latin America. Or stepfamilies can celebrate the first snowfall (or first flower of spring) in a unique, family way.

Special dates in the life of the stepfamily can also be celebrated in prayer and ritual. Consider, for example, a family celebration of the wedding anniversary or an annual remembrance of the first night the stepfamily came together in a home of their own.

Consciously choosing dates and events to celebrate that are different from those already being celebrated can help build new relationships (without denying the old) and build a pool of shared experiences and fun times to help families move forward into the future.

ENRICHING FAMILY RELATIONSHIPS

Families encourage the individual growth of family members and the development of meaningful relationships within and beyond the family. This is done when:

- parents grow in their understanding of the parenting skills needed at each stage of the family life cycle;
- families work to improve their communications, decision-making and problem-solving skills;
- families work at and enjoy spending quality time together;
- families participate in intergenerational, family activities which build community among family members and between families in the parish community;
- married couples consciously work at enriching their marriage relationship;
- single, divorced, separated or widowed adults work at enriching their lives and relationships through programs, support groups and resources that address their specific needs;
- families seek support and counseling during times of loss, sudden change, unexpected crises, problems and family or personal transitions.

The following activities provide practical examples of how family relationships can be nurtured and enriched in families with young adolescents.

ACTIVITY 1. HOLDING SUCCESSFUL FAMILY MEETINGS

The purpose of a family meeting is to discuss a variety of topics related to the family or its members. The most important reasons to hold family meetings are to share your lives and improve communication. The only way to guarantee

STRATEGIES AND ACTIVITIES

you will spend enough time together as a family is to make your time together a priority. By holding regular family meetings—even if they only last 15 minutes—you can find out what's happening in each other's lives and shape family time to respond to one another's needs.

Some important benefits of holding family meetings are:

- You save time because you can talk to everyone at once. You don't need to hunt down one family member at a time to inform them of an event or to ask his or her opinion on a family matter.

- Everyone will be motivated about a decision if they are allowed to have some input into the decisions.

- The meetings help demonstrate good decision-making skills.

- Family meetings are an excellent time to recognize the accomplishments each family member has made. With so little time in households, often only problems are addressed.

- Communication is improved. The more opportunity your family has to share opinions, ideas, and thoughts, the better you will understand each other and the better you will get along.

It is a good idea to plan the first few, until both you and your children understand the structure of the meetings. Eventually, you can have meetings in the car, after dinner or whenever everyone happens to be together. The larger your family, the more difficult it is to find a time when everyone is free. Large families may have to schedule a set time each week. Perhaps there is a time each week when your family is together anyway, like Sunday dinner. This would be a good time to hold a meeting. Hold your meetings whenever and wherever you can. The important thing is for everyone to be together.

Planned or spontaneous, serious or light, family meetings are a way to improve communication and spend more time together. To get the most out of your family meetings:

- Begin your meeting with something positive. Try to make a complimentary remark about each person.
- Set rules and make sure you follow them. One good rule for every meeting is, "No interrupting."
- Be flexible. Even if you've planned a topic for discussion, if something more important comes up, discuss that instead.
- Let adolescents have a say in family issues. Adolescents feel better about themselves and are more likely to be happy with decisions if they feel they have some input.
- Set reasonable limits for the choices that have to be made.
- Stick to the issues being discussed.
- Be careful when discussing personal or embarrassing issues.
- Follow up. Make sure everyone understands why certain decisions have been made and how they are to follow new rules. In two-parent families, parents should be sure they agree with each other on the decision made.

All family members need to practice a few skills in order to have successful family meetings:
- paying attention;
- participating in conversation;
- giving and accepting criticism;
- disagreeing calmly;
- giving and accepting compliments;
- accepting decisions.

[Adapted from: *Take Time to be a Family: Holding Successful Family Meetings*. Boys Town Videos for Parents; available from Don Bosco Multimedia]

ACTIVITY 2. KIDS AND CONTRACTS— NEGOTIATING WITHIN THE FAMILY

Parents and young adolescents often have different opinions on how family responsibilities should be shared or family policies enforced. A contract is simply a written statement of what your child agrees to do and what the consequences are if he or she accomplishes the goal. Writing contracts is an excellent tool for helping young adolescents set and reach goals. Using a contract approach to negotiate family differences can help improve family communications, build young people's self esteem and strengthen their commitment to the goals agreed upon together.

The Steps

1) Identify the goal: Through discussion, come to a common understanding of the problem and one or more approaches you can take to solve it. The approaches or goals you come up with together should be specific, measurable and realistic.

A goal, for example, of "helping more around the house" is too general. Narrow it down to be a specific, measurable goal such as taking responsibility for meal clean up on two specific nights each week.

2) Write the contract together: In addition to writing down the goal you have agreed on together, and the consequences, set a time limit. If the goal is a long-term one, set regular check-in times to assess progress toward the established goal.

Consequences, both positive and negative, should be proportional to the goal accomplished. Consequences should not automatically include opening your wallet. Rewards for accomplishing a goal can include having a friend spend the night, getting a later curfew or going out for pizza.

After the contract is written, date it and sign it together. Then place it where it will be noticed during the day.

3) Follow-up: Once the contract is written, provide encouragement and review the progress your son or daughter is making. It is crucial that young adolescents know you are aware of the effort being made and appreciate it.

If your child isn't able to reach the original goal, or if it becomes obvious during the week that the contract is too difficult or unclear, write a new contract that will be achievable.

Here is a sample contract that families can adapt for their own use:

DATE:

We, _____, _____ (parent's name/children's names) agree to the following.

GOALS

1. I _____ (child's name) will study for at least one hour every evening, Sunday through Thursday before asking to go out or watch TV.

2. I _____ (child's name) will start my homework assignments at 5:00 p.m. each day and work on them until they're completed.

CONSEQUENCES

1. If I complete steps 1 and 2 for each day of the week, I get an extended curfew for organized activities with friends on Friday or Saturday night.

2. If I do not complete steps 1 and 2 each day, I will not be allowed to take part in such activities.

_____ (Child)

_____ (Parent)

Conclusion

Do not use contract writing only when there is a problem in your home. If you do, your young adolescent may begin to see problem behavior as a way to get rewards through writing a contract. Use it just as often to help him or her accomplish personal goals in school, with friends or in sports.

Learn More About It:

Negotiating Within the Family. Boys Town Video for Parents. The 15-minute video is available from Don Bosco Multimedia.

ACTIVITY 3. ENRICHING RELATIONSHIPS IN BLENDED FAMILIES

Families today come in different sizes, shapes and configurations. Many young people live at least a portion of their lives in blended families, sharing their home with one biological parent, a step parent and a mixture of biological and step siblings. Blended families are a special and different kind of family. While parents and youth in blended families are similar in some ways to parents and youth in other kinds of families, their journey can also be quite different. Adults who carry the dual role of biological and stepparent can feel like jugglers—attempting to develop new relationships with stepchildren while nurturing established relationships with their biological offspring. Young people in blended families can feel alone, or conversely, overwhelmed by their struggle to maintain relationships with two, three or four different parents. In *Strengthening Your Stepfamily*, Elizabeth Einstein and Linda Albert suggest the following guidelines for easing the adjustment of parents into stepfamily life:

For stepparents:

- Seek support—from your spouse, friends, minister or rabbi, other stepparents.
- Be there for your stepchildren, but allow them time to learn to trust and respect you.
- Respect the strong bond that exists between your spouse and children. Allow them plenty of time together and avoid interfering where issues are not your concern.

For biological parents:

- Include your new spouse in your existing family unit, but let relationships develop at their own pace.
- Be supportive, ready to listen and discuss difficulties.
- Encourage a cooperative spirit between your spouse and the children's other biological parent.

For both of you:

- Explore your parenting styles and take classes together to develop problem-solving and discipline skills.
- Work out ways for your stepfamily to communicate: family meetings, bulletin boards, complaint and compliment pots, regular planned activities.
- Talk about feelings. Airing them aloud diminishes their power.
- Be patient, allowing plenty of time for family members to work through their many differences.
- Make your couple relationship a priority. Remember, when parents are happy, children feel more secure.

Learn More About It:

Bonkowski Ph.D., Sara. *Teens Are NON Divorceable.* Chicago: ACTA Publications, 1990.

Clubb, Angela Neumann. *Love in the Blended Family.* Deerfield Beach, FL: Health Communications, Inc., 1991.

Einstein, Elizabeth and Linda Albert. *Strengthening Your Stepfamily.* Circle Pines, MN: American Guidance Service, 1986.

Getzoff, Ann and Carolyn McClenahan. *Step Kids: A Survival Guide for Teenagers in Step Families.* New York: Walker and Company, 1984.

RESPONDING TO THOSE IN NEED AND RELATING TO THE WIDER COMMUNITY

Families respond to the gospel call to service by reaching out in compassion to those in need. This is done when:

- family members model the gospel values of respect for human dignity, compassion, justice and service to others in their relationships with each other and with others in the community;
- families learn about justice issues and the needs of others;
- family members participate together in parish and community service programs geared to their interests and abilities;
- families discuss how the needs of others, locally and globally, affect their life as a family;
- families joins with others in society to alleviate the suffering of those in need and change the structures that allow injustice and inequality to continue.

Families work to better understand the world they live in and make it a better place for all people. This is done when:

- families model hospitality, opening their home to others, showing how God's love is communicated through family life;
- families grow in appreciation of their own ethnic or cultural heritage;
- families takes part in parish and community events that help them understand the life and history of people of different cultures and nations, and value cultural diversity as a special gift from God;

- families recognize their connectedness with and reliance upon others at all levels of life and grow in their appreciation for interdependence;
- families learn about and join in actions with others who share a common vision and approach for improving life in the community.

The following activities provide examples of how the families with young adolescents can reach out together in response to the needs of the local and wider community.

ACTIVITY 1. FAMILY FINANCES

Talk through finances regularly so that all family members have a better idea about what is involved in budgeting and how much things really cost. Decide how and when major purchases will be made. Discuss together how the family shares its resources with others, how much of the family income goes to church, charitable and social change groups and how the money is divided.

ACTIVITY 2. A HANDS-ON APPROACH TO FAMILY SERVICE

For many young adolescents, "who I am" is defined largely in terms of "what I do." Involving them as family members in hands-on service to others helps them to understand that service is integral to who we are as Christian families and as church.

Explore the possibilities for volunteer service with local soup kitchens and homeless shelters, hospitals and community service organizations.

Choose, as a family, a service project and site that best fits your schedule and abilities.

STRATEGIES AND ACTIVITIES 85

Prepare together for your service involvement, learning what you need to know to be comfortable at the work site.

Do the project together, working as a family unit or in pairs, helping each other as needed.

Share. When the project is finished, debrief it together, sharing the highs and lows of the experience, your thoughts and feelings, and your suggestions for making the experience better next time around.

Pray. Finally, bring your family experience to prayer, offering simple petitions of thanksgiving or need for what you learned about yourself and others through the experience and, especially for the gift you are to one another as a family.

Learn More About It:

Lewis, Barbara A. *The Kid's Guide to Social Action.* Minneapolis: Free Spirit Publishing Inc., 1991.
McGinnis, Kathleen and James. *Parenting for Peace and Justice.* Maryknoll, NY: Orbis Books, 1981.
Salzman, Marian and Teresa Reisgies. *150 Ways Teens Can Make a Difference.* Princeton, NJ: Peterson's Guides, Inc., 1991.

ACTIVITY 3. ALTERNATIVE FAMILY VACATION

Plan an "alternative" family vacation this year. Take part as a family in a cultural immersion program or a work camp experience.

For information on immersion and work camp experiences check with your diocesan family life, youth or mission office. Check, too, with missionary groups working in your area or national self-help groups like Habitat for Humanity. Still other groups may be organized around a common concern for the environment.

ACTIVITY 4. JUSTICE ISSUES AS PLAYED OUT IN THE NEWS AND POPULAR MEDIA

Use the justice issues played out in daily newscasts or newspapers as a springboard for helping young people discover what they think about, or how they might react to similar situations in their own lives. A rash of stories or articles on sexual harassment in the work place offers parents an opportunity to share the stories or questions they have about the issue. It can serve, as well, as an opportunity for young people to look at how well they incorporate their own beliefs into their relationships with others at home, at school and at work.

If you are watching the evening news together, ask what your son or daughter thinks about the situation being described. Raise questions about causes, consequences and the options open to the people involved in the story reported. Move beyond the questions of who, what and when to the issues of why and how. Discuss, for example: Why did people respond as they did? What values are at stake in the story? How could things have been handled differently? How might you react in a similar situation?

Talk through an issue of local, national or global injustice from your local newspaper or a news magazine, over a meal or at any other convenient time. Let your child know what you think and why, without expecting him or her to mouth exactly the same sentiments. Talking the issues through together with respect for one another's thoughts and opinions is far more important than agreeing on all the details.

Popular media (music and movies, television programs and video games) provide abundant examples of justice issues that demand a considered response from Christians. Here too, the process of dialogue is far more important than the ultimate decision.

ACTIVITY 5. REASSESSING FAMILY ROLES AND RESPONSIBILITIES

As a family, keep track of how family responsibilities are shared at home (who does what, how often, how long).

After a month, evaluate what the list tells you about family roles and responsibilities. What criteria is used for deciding who does what—gender, talent, availability, desire, sharing the tough stuff evenly? Are family tasks shared justly? Why or why not?

Try out a new configuration of sharing tasks around home for a month or two, then sit down again to evaluate how well the system is working.

Young people's involvement in seasonal sports and extracurricular activities often means that some months are overcrowded while others are thin on outside commitments. Reassessing family responsibilities on a regular basis can help keep everyone attuned to what is going on in family member's lives and create a bit more openness to "going the extra mile" with household tasks when it is needed.

ACTIVITY 6. EATING FOR A WEEK ON A FOOD STAMPS BUDGET

Plan your meal menu a week or month in advance as a family, then shop together for the food you need. Keep your meal budget to $1.65 or less per person per day—the financial allotment provided to families that receive U.S. Government food stamps. As you eat your simple meals (and refrain from eating sneaky snacks on the side) think about and pray for those for whom this exercise is an ongoing necessity. Let the activity flow naturally into a discussion of the extent and causes of poverty locally and in the country.

ACTIVITY 7. MULTICULTURAL CONNECTIONS: COMBINE FUN WITH LEARNING ABOUT OTHERS

Use holidays and vacation trips to open up your family to different cultural and ethnic experiences. Select from the following ideas:

- Take part in ethnic festivals and celebrations in your local community.
- Visit a restaurant that features ethnic cuisine, or celebrate an ethnic night at home, involving the entire family in deciding on a menu and helping with food preparation.
- Check on the availability of art shows, musical performances and other local events that can expose your family to the customs, traditions and talents of the ethnic or cultural groups that make up your part of the state or country.
- Subscribe to magazines and periodicals that feature stories about people from different parts of the world. *National Geographic World*, for example, is great for the primary school set. A family subscription to *National Geographic* or a justice magazine like *Seeds* or *Sojourners* can fulfill the same purpose with older adolescents.

The more varied and multicultured their experiences are while still at home, the more comfortable children will be as they move out into the varied and multicultured society that the U.S. is today.

ACTIVITY 8. PUTTING ROOTS ON YOUR FAMILY TREE

Connecting with an appropriate holiday or celebration (Thanksgiving, All Souls Day, ethnic/national holiday, birthday or anniversary) develop a family tree that goes back

STRATEGIES AND ACTIVITIES

three, four or five generations. List people's names and birth dates, occupations and interests, places of birth and residence. Use the activity as a way of celebrating who you are as a family, your connectedness with people of other times and places, and your membership in an interdependent world community.

ACTIVITY 9. PEN PALS, TAPE MATES OR VIDEO BUDDIES

Learn about the people and customs of other countries by adopting a pen pal. If letter writing is not your strength, individually or as a family, find a tape mate or video buddy. Swap photos of each other's neighborhood and home, school and parish, family and friends. Explore the resources of your library and local bookstores to learn more about the history and customs of your new friend's country. Claim one of his or her national celebrations as a family event, incorporating whatever you can by way of food and music, decorations and dress. Display your new friend's picture in your home. Add him or her and the needs of his country to your prayer.